Human Resource Management in Libraries

Piyush Kanti Mahapatra

Ess Ess Publications

4837/24, Ansari Road, Darya Ganj,
New Delhi-110002
✆ : 3260807, 3201533
Fax : 3274173
E-mail: essess@del3.vsnl.net.in
url:http://www.essessbooks.com

First Published 2002

ISBN : 81-7000-323-7

Rs. 650/-

Published by:

Ess Ess Publications

4837/24, Ansari Road, Darya Ganj,
New Delhi - 110 002
Phone : 3260807
Fax : 3274173
E-mail : essess@del3.vsnl.net.in
url: http://www.essessbooks.com

Laser Typesetting:
Mukesh Graphics
L-2/8, Mangolepuri, New Delhi
Ph.:7924405

Printed at :
Print Line

Contents

Contents

Preface

Human resource management in libraries is on the crossroads. Human resource has never been so necessary as key resource. The challenges facing modern library and information services demand learning, information systems and services, speed, responsiveness and capability. The demands can be fulfilled only by persons with good academic background, professional skills, expertise, leadership for accomplishment of the library activities and operations. The united efforts of the work force can fulfil the objectives of the library and achieve the goals of the organisation. The individuals with the teamwork can accomplish what is meant to do, in short, organisational capabilities. Human resource management is uniquely positioned to deliver organisational capabilities in the era of technological innovations by assuming an entirely new role and developing a new agenda.

Human resource management is relatively a new term used in industry and business areas. Personnel management and human resource management are not synonymous. Human resource management is a concept and approach to shape the organisational work culture, and in libraries it is service-oriented. Human resource management is basically the development and administration of personnel policies and procedures, but managing people also entails proper understanding of the psychological and sociological forces that affect the attitudes and performances of individuals as well as the groups as work force. The library personnel are heterogeneous, consisting of individuals of varying ages, levels of education, areas of expertise, differing motivation, personal characteristics, aspirations, needs and personalities. The library management must understand how these factors interact in the work environment.

Library management should consider the factors which improve the functional aspects and develop personal qualities for best personal contributions. The purpose of human resource management is to motivate, train, encourage, educate and guide the library personnel for accomplishment of the goals of the organisation. It is also important to judge and evaluate every person as individual because all the persons are not alike. Library management has to evaluate every person regarding one's inherent qualities and performance as well as to guide the persons to attain the desired levels of capabilities.

Chapter 1 deals with the principles of human resource management and their objectives with a discussion on human resource development climate. Chapter 2 discusses various aspects of human resource management. Chapter 3 presents the changing concept of new leadership, fission approach to fusion approach - a new management paradigm in which the individuals and organisations can grow together by imbibing subtle forces of mind. Chapter 4 deals with motivation factor, an important aspect of human resource. Chapter 5 notes the importance of communication flows as well as barriers to communication. Chapters 6 and 7 emphasise needs and implementation of training and new employee orientation. Chapters 8 and 9 highlight collaborative teamwork and effective meetings. Chapter 10 mentions the necessity of performance evaluation.

Chapter 11 discusses management leadership, its qualities and roles of management leaders. Chapter 12 emphasises the human resource strategies, the workforce and strategic planning. Chapter 13 highlights the learning support systems in electronic environment and global perspective.

The library management is facing ever-increasing challenges both administrative and academic. The volume of knowledge and its management are getting overwhelming. Human resource management is one aspect of management but the most crucial and vital one. If it is done properly, the library will grow and develop, otherwise the organisation, as a whole, will not achieve the goals.

I am grateful to Mrs. Sheel Sethi of Ess Ess Publications, New Delhi, for her encouragement and cooperation for the publication of the book.

Author

1

Human Resource : Principles

All the library activities, functions and operations are done by people whether these are manual or in the electronic system. Behind all the planning, designing, organisation, implementation and performing results, there is the human mind. The motivation, endeavours, accomplishment, service to users, fulfiling the objectives and achieving the goals of the library depend only on the people who work in the library with their mind, performance, cooperation and support. Every person is master of his own job with motivation, direction, challenge and accomplishment. A library requires many kinds of resources but the human resource is at the zenith of all other resources.

As the leader of the organisation the librarian has the special responsibility to plan, organise and direct the workforce so that the library can achieve the goals and accomplish what it is meant for. There are some methods and systems for human resource management and also some general theories. There are some rules, regulations and procedures in all the libraries. There are all the guidelines for directing the workforce. These printed guidelines and verbal instructions are thought to be the instruments for managing people. Obviously, these are essential but rules and regulations only cannot manage people. All the persons may not work as desired by these rules. Rules cannot be applied to all human endeavours. The behavioural patterns of persons differ. These may not have predictable effect on all the persons. People may work strictly according to rules and regulations but the output and result may not reach the desired and expected performance level.

There are some additional factors which improve the functional aspects and develop personal qualities leading to best personal contributions. The human resource managers must give emphasis on these factors. For this purpose the managers must understand each person as individual, his attitude, motivation, knowledge, skill, proficiency, expertise, and even liking. It must be accepted that individuals are different. The basic principles of human resource management are to motivate the people, to get the best contribution from the individuals, to initiate them to achieve success, to make them feel at home with the organisation, and to create a sense of belonging to the library.

The general requirements of the library personnel are almost identical in all the libraries as well as all the people employed in a particular library at various levels of professional qualification experience, skills, expertise, proficiency in job accomplishment, and such other requirements are almost equal for different professional positions. But all the people having the same qualifications and experience also do not behave and work in the same way. Here comes the question of human factors.

The individuals make the difference. The role of the library and the fulfilments of obligations depend very much on the role and performance of the library personnel.

Individual employee performs particular tasks or activities. Accomplishment of one's tasks is not only the responsibilities of one individual, but it also support the activities of the library as an organisation. If an individual does not perform his tasks, it is not only the failure of the individual, it affects the activities of the library. At the same time, it affects the job performance of other individuals also. On the other hand, if an employee is motivated, takes the job performance as a challenge and his attitude is positive, he can be a source of inspiration to other co-workers. Library operations are done in a linear order following a chain system. Therefore, individual's performance affects the work schedule of other individuals as well as of the library.

An organisation runs with the people involved in the organisational set up and the persons involved are not only individual units performing their jobs in social isolation. Individuals in an organisation create social clusters within which professional and social support develop. People work in a cohesive manner with proper cooperation and coordination. In libraries the employees are part of a complex network of interrelated functions to achieve the goals of the organisation. The motivation and positive role of the employees are the foundation stone of the library's success. It has also an environmental impact. Performance of the human resource of a library creates its image in the society.

The objectives of human resource management are to motivate, encourage, train, educate and guide the library personnel to accomplish the goals of the organisation in the most effective way. Human resource management creates conditions in which all the people are guided, directed and developed to get best of their services. For this purpose, it is also important to judge and evaluate every person as individual because all the persons are not alike. Individuals have their own strength and weakness, ability and inability, worthiness and unworthiness, motivation and negligence to a certain degree. The human resource managers have to evaluate every individual regarding their performance and inherent qualities. They should prepare and guide them to attain the desired level of capability.

Human resource management and personnel management - these two terms are not synonymous. Human resource management is not just personnel management, it is a concept and approach to shape the organisational work culture and to fulfil the objectives of the library and achieving the goals of the organisation. All these can be done by the planned human resource in the library by motivating the persons to work in an environment of participation, cooperation and collaboration. In such work environment personal qualities, qualifications, skills, efficiency and other attributes will be recognised, best performance will be rewarded, but all the persons in the library will work as units of the organisation to achieve the goals.

Human resource is vital and crucial because all other resources in the library cannot be acquired and utilised without human resource. The employees of the library, existing or new entrants, should be turned as asset and all kinds of resources should be utilised to the optimum level. The management of human resource takes care of the enhancement of capabilities of every individual employee as well as utilisation of the potentialities of individuals. Individual employees have their own roles and they should have their group roles. The functions of human resource management include enhancement of capabilities of individuals required to perform individual tasks, placement of individual employees in the right positions and development of organisational culture through inter personal relationships, hierarchical and lateral.

Development of human resource should be done through guidance, counselling, training, performance appraisal, organisational development, career development and exploring personal potentialities.

HUMAN RESOURCE DEVELOPMENT CLIMATE

The human resource development climate of the library plays a vital role in ensuring the competency, motivation and development of the employees. The term 'climate' is used to designate the quality of the work environment in cooperation, development of individual, dedication and commitment of individuals to organisational goals, and the efficiency with which the goals are achieved. Such climate can be created not only by formal control system but also through informal intrapersonal relationships. Both the formal and informal structures of human resource management create the organisational climate. In such condition individuals assist, help, judge, reward, restrain, guide, counsel, and feel each other. The climate influences attitudes and morale of individuals towards their activities and work environment.

D. Hellriegel and J.W. Slocum define organisational climate as a "set of attributes which can be perceived about a particular organisation and/or its sub-systems, and that may be induced in the way that organisation and/or its sub-systems deal with their members and environment." Another definition has been given by B. Schneider as "Climate perceptions are psychologically meaningful molar descriptions that people can agree characterize a system's practices and procedures. By its practices and procedures a system may create many climates. People perceive climates because the molar perceptions function as frames of reference for the attainment of some congruity between behaviour and the system's practices and procedures.

However, if the climate is one which rewards and supports individual differences, people in the same system will not behave similarly. Further, because satisfaction is a personal evaluation of a system's practices and procedures, people in the system tend to agree less on their satisfaction than on their description of the system's climate."

Human resource development climate is an integral part of organisational culture. The employees should have a developmental environment in the organisation. The elements of human resource development climate are given below:

* All the library personnel should be treated as the most important resource,
* Competence of the employees must be developed,
* There should be free communication, discussion and exchange of opinion and ideas,
* Efforts should be made to help employees recognise their strengths and weaknesses through feedback,
* There should be trust in the capabilities of the employees that they can acquire new competence at any stage of service period,
* There should be environment of cooperation, collaboration and cohesiveness,
* Team spirit should be the guiding force,
* Acceptance of modern technology in library operations,
* Stereotype jobs and favouritism should be discouraged,
* Human resource development services should be a continuing process such as, job-rotaion, assignment planning reward management, performance evaluation, training, etc.

A supportive climate is essential for human resource development if it has to be implemented effectively. Top management to immediate supervisors should have the commitment for positive attitudes towards development. Human resource development climate creates the organisational work culture.

There should be openness so that all the library personnel can feel free to discuss, exchange and communicate their ideas, feelings and activities with each other. Whenever there is any problem, it should be confronted and solved, and should not be kept shelved. Mutual trust should be there in working relationships for the benefit of the library. Persons should be allowed to work independently with responsibility and the results should be monitored. Initiative should be encouraged. In the situations where team work in necessary, collaborative efforts should be taken.

PLANNING AND IMPLEMENTATION

Planning and implementation of human resource management are essential for acquiring and improving capabilities required to perform various functions for the present and also for the future. Planning should be made to develop individual capabilities and discover inner potential for personal and organisational improvement. By this way the organisational culture can be created and maintained through interpersonal relationships at various levels, collaboration, professional expertise and human resource development climate. Library personnel should be supported to acquire new competencies through a process of performance planning, periodic review of performance, monitoring, assessment of development needs and creation of development opportunities through assignment responsibilities, training, rewarding and such other mechanisms.

Performance competencies, knowledge, attitudes and values, skills and expertise are needed to achieve the best results. Higher degree of performing tasks and better quality of results require higher level or degree of skills and expertise as well as utilisation of human resource in the most effective way. Properly motivated, competent and responsible employees are the asset of the organisation for organisational survival, growth and excellence. Proper utilisation of human resource can overcome the constraints of all other kinds of resources.

Human resource development must be a continuing process in the libraries. Planning and implementation of the human resource development are activated by human resource development mechanisms, climate and processes leading to the outcomes and best results. The mechanism, climate and processes create more competent and committed persons who would make the library grow by contributing their best to the library. Human resource management influences very much the organisational effectiveness.

Human resource development mechanisms are the planning for human resource management, assessment of existing position or posts, identification of vacant and new positions with requirements to perform the tasks, reorganisation of positions and demand for new intake, system analysis and flow charts, task identifications and job descriptions, role analysis exercise, potential development exercises, communication policies, organisational development exercises, job-enriched programmes, job rotation, and other mechanisms.

Human resource development processes include

planning of development by every employee, awareness of competencies required for job performance, proactive orientation, collaboration and team work, mutual trust, authenticity in attitudes and activities, openness, motivation to take challenge, value generation, clarification of norms and standards, increased communication, fulfilment of objectives, role clarity, completion of jobs and tasks within stipulated time frame, efficiency in job performance, work motivation, better generation of internal resources, better utilisation of human resources, higher work commitment and job involvement, more team work, respect for each other, personal and team performance, and the like.

The outcomes and results will be more competent human resource, better developed roles, higher service satisfaction, growth and diversification, cost reduction, organisational effectiveness and better image. Mechanism, processes and outcomes are closely inter related and these are a continuing process within the library. There should be some persons to think constantly on planning and implementation, to assess the extent to which these are being achieved, and to keep reviewing and evaluating. Continuous performance appraisal has two approaches, evaluation approach and development approach and these two approaches are complementary.

INDIVIDUALS

The major objective of human resource management is to increase the individual employee's effectiveness with additional objectives which will give each employee an increased sense of personal motivation and satisfaction in the work and the work environment. The most important point that has to be considered in dealing with the personnel is how they feel about their work, their co-workers, their supervisors, and the organisation for which they work.

The principles of human resource management should be implemented for the fulfilment of this end. Management must provide the leadership which will create effective coordination and utilisation of both human and other resources towards the achievement of the goals of the library. Organisation and motivation of the personnel is the control function of human resource management. It is important how the employees are viewed by their superiors, the way they are dealt with, the way in which they perceive their own roles, and the way in which they relate to co-workers as well as users of the library.

In case of new positions careful personnel selection using every device and technique should be made. It is to be ensured that each person selected is suited to the position for the work to be assigned immediately as well as for the future. The devices and techniques utilised to accomplish good selection include carefully prepared job descriptions, appropriate tests, interviews, well-developed applications, evaluation of experience information, educational qualifications, assessment of skills and expertise in specific areas required.

Job descriptions and specifications are an absolute necessity to get best results. If the job requires a particular personality or set of psychological traits, such factors must be considered during selection process. Evaluation of prospective employees is indispensable in making sure that they are physically, mentally and temperamentally suited to the job they will do. There should not be any confusion as to assignments and responsibilities. The person who clearly understand an assignment is the right person. Persons must have responsibility for doing something in the work process. They should have single accountability to provide functional responsibility.

Human resource can be best utilised by appreciation of the individual for the result-oriented performance. If a person feels that his contribution is significant and his efficiency and productivity is acknowledged, he will be motivated to perform his jobs in a better way with right attitude and dedication. Such positive attitude brings a sense of worthiness to the work. The supervisors must encourage and inspire the staff to show initiative in thinking and executing plans. Subordinates should be allowed to exercise initiative within the limits provided by their job assignments and responsibilities.

The employees should have pride in their accomplishments. If they feel a sense of pride in objectives, methods and accomplishments, better performance can be expected and a reasonable degree of dedication will prevail. The supervisors should follow the principle of clearly defining objectives and outcomes expected, communicating these to the staff, and recognising achievements when assignments are well done. Supervisors should use praise as a tool of motivation. Good performance and sincerity should be rewarded with praise.

The employees need to have information on programmes, events and actions affecting them or in which they have an interest. Good support and high motivation can be assured by making certain that all employees are adequately informed about the matters concerned. Information sharing can be an effective means of staff motivation. Management must give careful and thoughtful consideration to the administrative steps to be taken and their effect on the feelings and performance of staff members. This is especially true when considering changes in procedures, programmes, activities and services.

Participation in the planning, organising and

implementing decisions can be a strong tool of motivation. It creates better relationships with and among employees. The greater employee participation in decision-making and policy development help the management in many ways. The employees will follow instructions from higher authority and accept them more readily when they have contributed to the decisions and policy statements upon which such instructions are based.

The physical facilities, communication system, quality of equipment, infrastructural facilities and working conditions provided for an employee on the job are highly important factors in achieving efficiency and high productivity. Better working conditions, both physical and psychological, ensure more efficiency and more productivity with the same amount of human effort.

2

HUMAN RESOURCE MANAGEMENT

The purpose of management is to accomplish the objectives of an organisation as quickly as possible at the lowest cost achieving highest performance standard. At many times the goals and objectives may shift and procedures of achieving the goals may change but ultimately the purpose of the organisation must be served most efficiently. In an organisation people tend to make thing more complicated than they are by paying too much attention to details and by following conventional procedures considering inchangeable. It is better to create a total framework that supports a body of work. The elements that are common to an area of performance should be identified for quick achievement of results in that endeavour. In any endeavour basic skills must be developed in the incremental way by training and education as continuing process to achieve highest performance.

Human resource is essentially the most important resource in the library. If the library personnel are rightly motivated, adequately qualified, sincere in their work, serious to achieve the result-oriented targets and feel a sense of belonging to the organisation, they can be regarded as the best resource of the library in comparison to all other physical resources. The human resource can only overcome the constraints and limitations of other physical resources. For these reasons the selection and appointment of library personnel should be in accordance with the jobs and responsibilities required in the library. The right person should be in the right situation for the right job requirement. The persons must have the expertise to perform the jobs. They should also be trained properly for the situations as and when required.

At the planning and management level a library system must have a well-defined, well-structured and realistic manpower policy considering both the routine jobs and developmental programmes. The organisational design and staff structure should facilitate the understanding of the role of individual, responsibilities to be discharged, adequate communication channels and group involvement in the system. All the members of the library staff must be kept informed of the factors affecting their work situations and they should be given opportunities to make useful contribution to the general functioning of the library.

HUMAN RESOURCE PLANNING

Effective human resource planning is a crucial job in the library system. The planning should consider both the existing staff as well as new intake. A clear understanding of the objectives, quantification of the performance of jobs, job specification and job analysis and agreement over the minimum deployment of staffing consistent with the desired and planned work situation are involved in the staffing pattern of the library. The collection of data for job specification and job analysis, preparation of flow charting for various operations, system analysis for the library operations at various stages, their subsequent interpretation, quantification and translating into manpower requirement are extremely difficult in library situation. In case of certain library operations, such as accessioning, classification, cataloguing, circulation of books, and the like, can be made by quantification and measurement. But reference services, readers guidance, maintenance of catalogue and databases, current awareness services, information services, referral services, and the like, cannot be measured by time and job specification. In different kinds of libraries the work situation may vary and norms for measurement cannot be applied in the same way. In such situations the objectives and goals of the library and the performance to achieve these through implementation of services should be considered.

In any changed situation, particularly under library automation programmes all the conventional library departments have to be reconstituted, all the activities have to be redesigned and all the library operations have to be reorganised. Library automation system requires totally new job specifications and job analysis, new work situation, electronic environment, new operational procedures and new techniques of management and communication. The work environment requires a new generation of library personnel, whether in-service or new recruits, dedicated to achieve the goals. Motivation to accept the challenges in library operation is the guiding force to success.

In staff participation the manager concerned must be in full control of all the jobs and he must be fully prepared for all the activities of his unit. His involvement will inspire the commitment of the subordinate and it must be self-generated. It will grow as the programmes for activities are implemented. At every stage of implementation upward consultation will be required in which both the parties are motivated. Thus, the subordinate is motivated to make the job done properly and the manager is motivated to develop the participation involved.

Staff participation may be achieved by the management technique of Management by Objectives (Mb0). In this particular technique the departmental and unit objectives are to be established as the first step. These will be done by the management at the top level. At the same time the key areas of activities are to be undertaken and the methods of implementation should be considered. The steps in the system may be described as follows:

1. Fact finding, review of the existing situation and identifying the weakness of operation in case of unit working, or fact finding and justification of establishing a new unit for activity.
2. Setting objectives and planning for the organisation.
3. Setting objectives of the department or unit.
4. Blending long-term and short-term plans.
5. Identifying key areas of activity.
6. Operating and improvement planning.
7. Development of criteria to judge performance.
8. Creating enthusiasm and participation in achieving results.
9. Removing obstacles, revising programme when necessary.
10. Regular review of progress and performance.
11. Involvement of all the individuals in activity and end-result.
12. Review of total result for all the staff.

At every step there must be action review, control and monitoring over all the operational activities. All these should be done in cooperation with the employees and with their active participation. It is essential at all the stages of activity and the progress should be measured in a continuing manner.

B.G. Dutton has described some criteria to measure the progress. These are :

"1. Adoption of individual targets - deep knowledge of areas of technology, information services, languages, etc.

2. Definition of training needs - having established individual objectives, staff were encouraged to select meetings, courses, etc. to promote relevant expertise and subsequently to pass on information gained at in-house seminars. This proved a good taste of their own understanding.

3. Extent to which all aspects of work are subject to self-examination.

4. Openness in discussing and solving problems.

5. Elimination of unnecessary work, e.g., by identification and justification of the least important tasks done. Excessive checking is often detected here.

6. Acceptance of more exacting work - shortening lines of communications through effective delegations with decision-taking nearer the sources of information and action.

7. More optimal use of mechanized methods."

On one hand, there are increasing financial constraints, limitation of physical resources, exorbitant price rise for books and journals, enhancement of cost of furniture and equipment, non-availability of adequate number of posts required for ever-increasing workload, and on the other hand, increasing number of users, a wide variety of materials they require, changing patterns of their needs and requirements, various types of new services to be introduced in the library, ever-increasing demanding nature of the users requirements, impact of technological innovations in modern library situations - all these conditions have put the library management in a very different and challenging situation. The librarian can overcome such situations by proper library planning, taking result-oriented programmes, efficient financial control, and above all, meaningful human resource planning and management. Every person in the library must be motivated, dedicated and efficient in job performance. Manpower planning and human resource management are essential elements to achieve the goals.

In libraries, therefore, business management techniques in programme planning, budgeting, performance-orientation, system analysis and operation research have been adopted and have been found effective. The management of the library must monitor the performance of the library personnel to ensure that organisational expectations are fulfilled properly. If these are not met adequately, the library management should take corrective action. At the same time those whose performance is good enough should be rewarded adequately. The corrective actions include decisions on re-scheduling, transfers, reviews, promotion, new or changed assignments as well as decisions on warning, disciplinary actions etc. There may be some external factors which can affect the librarian's freedom to take corrective actions. Any library is a part of a larger parent organisation. Corrective decisions, therefore must be consistent with the policy of the parent organisation.

Employees union may also become a factor for collective interest. Legal rights of the employees may stand in the way. All these aspects should be considered while taking corrective action. It should be kept in mind that library is a service organisation having continuing operational activities.

LIBRARY PERSONNEL

There are three factors in any library. These are the materials, users and library personnel. Library materials are there for the users. The library personnel are responsible for organisation and arrangement of the library materials as well as for users services. Therefore, the operational activities of the library personnel are vital in the library. A library must have required number of competent, well-trained, qualified and motivated professionals and supporting staff according to the particular kind and size of the library.

Library is basically a repository of knowledge and store house of information as recorded in various types of library materials and information sources. The users require the information or the document according to their intellectual standard and capability in any branch of knowledge. The library personnel should have good academic background. Knowledge, professional qualification, awareness of information sources and technology, competence and an attitude to render service. The staffing pattern depends very much on the particular kind of the library, size of the library concerning the library holding having various types of documents and the number of users. The staffing framework should be planned and designed in a library on the basis of job analysis for smooth workflow, job description of individuals, activity analysis of a section or unit as well as activities of coordination, supervision and control. The total workload, the nature of jobs to be done, the services to be performed the development programmes to be undertaken and other related matters should be considered while designing the staffing framework and organisational chart. Flow charts of various operational units must be prepared to make the operational units properly activated and for functional coordination among the related operational units. The number of persons at the administrative position and number of persons at the operational levels should be considered keeping in view the hierarchical order according to the organisational chart.

The nature and quality of service of a library depend largely on the activities of library personnel. The wise collection development, proper organisation of knowledge and information sources by efficient technical processing, storage and retrieval of information, immediate availability of documents whenever asked for, reference and information service, bibliographical service, current awareness service, readers guidance, all these are performed by the workforce in the library, currently known as human resource. Only professional or technical training will not yield the best result unless the persons have the intellectual capability and sound academic knowledge with awareness of comprehensive information sources.

The library personnel should know the changing patterns of the modern documentary sources in different physical formats, the nature of the exponential growth of literature, the trends of development of various branches of knowledge, ramifications of the wide body of knowledge, emerging new subject areas, evaluation of appropriate information sources and changing needs and requirements of the users for very specific and highly specialised information. They must know also communication channels of information transfer, location of various types of databases and their availability, new technologies applied in library and information fields and global information resources.

Properly selected persons having sound academic knowledge, technical and professional expertise and motivation for library service having adequate experience only can perform the jobs rightly. The right persons for the proper positions should be selected. If required, they should go through orientation programmes and intensive in-service training to develop themselves to cope with the responsibilities assigned to them. In any library, continuing education should be the essential programme to keep the library personnel updated with latest developments in the profession and to acquire new expertise, particularly in the field of library automation and networking.

The basic activities of the library are making the documents accessible and available to users providing a wide range of library and information services. There are also very different types of activities not actually service to users but essentially supporting service to keep the library on-going. These are reprography, micrography, management of audiovisuals, binding, conservation of library materials, computer application, preparation of budget and financial control, accounting, convening meeting and keeping the records, organisation and maintenance of office records, routine jobs of office administration, and the like. Persons having qualifications and experience of performing such activities should be employed and trained in the library. Therefore, various types of persons should be there in different types of posts and positions.

The library personnel can be grouped in the following categories for various kinds of job requirements :

1. Professional of different grades for management and professional activities.
2. Semi-professionals for routine jobs.
3. Supporting staff for specified activities.
4. Staff for routing jobs in administration, financial work and accounts and other supporting services.

PROFESSIONALS

Professionals include persons employed at higher level and middle level responsible for administrative, managerial, professional and technical activities placed at supervisory positions. According to the organisational chart of a library the professionals are placed at various levels in the hierarchical order from top management level down to operational level upto a certain stage. Usually the librarian deputy librarians, assistant librarians and senior library assistants, whatever may be the designations, are included in this category. The senior professionals at top management level must have scholarship, comprehensive academic interest, adequate professional knowledge, technical expertise, knowledge of latest developments in the field and adequate experience. They will be responsible for identification of needs, analysis of problems, organisation of activities and operations, implementation of such works, inter-personal and inter-institutional communication and administering all the affairs of the library. They will also be responsible for setting the affairs of the library. They will also be responsible for setting the goals, defining the objectives, planning, programming and making creative solutions. They must have leadership role, must know motivation techniques and must be capable for directing the departments, divisions, personnel and the library as a whole.

SEMI PROFESSIONAL

The persons appointed as semi-professionals are placed at the lower level in the hierarchical order. They usually perform the routine professional and technical jobs. They should have qualifications in library and information science. They may be promoted to professional level after acquiring necessary qualification and experience. These jobs include book ordering, accessioning, preparation of books for the shelves, physical verification of the books, filing catalogue and shelf list cards, maintenance of catalogue and shelf list, circulation work, stock verification and rectification, keeping periodical records and many other routine jobs. Their designations may be library assistants, technical assistant, professional or information assistants, and the like.

SUPPORTING STAFF

The supporting staff include the persons with a wide range of skills from paraprofessional to administrative staff. A large number of routine and essential jobs are done by the supporting staff. These jobs may include many routine library jobs, jobs for reprography and micrography, handling and maintenance of audiovisual and other non-book materials, operation of different types of equipment, copying of various papers, preparation of accession lists, preventive jobs for preservation of library materials, stack room maintenance jobs, repairing and restoration of damaged books, book binding, maintenance of fumigation chambers, deacidification, lamination and other conservation jobs, and many other jobs. They must have minimum educational background but the most important factors are their professional and technical skill and adequate experience in doing particular trade or jobs. Since the jobs are of varied nature without having any relationship among them, persons must be employed who have adequate training, proven ability, experience and skill in a particular kind of job. The designations may be reprographic assistant, book binder, conservation assistant, and the like.

ADMINISTRATIVE AND ACCOUNTS STAFF

Adequate number of staff is required in a library for non-professional jobs. Their jobs are not specifically library jobs but they keep and maintain the infrastructural framework of the library. They also do a wide and varied kinds of jobs not necessarily related to each other. Persons with particular qualification and experience should be employed for various specific job requirements. The jobs include routine jobs relating to advertisement for appointment, interview, selection and appointment, promotion and retirement records, preparation of salary bills, leave records, keeping records of meetings, maintenance of files, and the like. The jobs also include inviting tenders, purchase, stores and supplies, printing and stationary, keeping correspondence records and various types of registers, receiving and dispatch, building maintenance, dusting and cleaning, security, canteen and other essential services. Several persons should be in the library for looking after the budget and financial control, accounts, holding of cash, maintaining accounts for audit, and the like. The posts may be designated as administrative officer, finance officer, superintendent, security officer, section officer, accountant, accounts officer, etc. as required in a library.

ASSESSMENT OF STAFF REQUIREMENT

As an organization a library is a combination of interacting components. The components may be divided as division or departments and these are divided as sections which are further divided in units. These components or divisions are created for particular type of activities. The jobs are done by individuals in the units. The jobs done in units are correlated in sections and these are further correlated in departmental activities. Thus, the activities of each and every component are interrelated with each other leading to fulfilling the functions of the library as a whole.

At the first stage the decisions are taken, the planning is made, programmes are defined, organisational set up is established, functions are stated, activities are identified and then the implementation work is done by individuals responsible for particular task or jobs. Therefore, the requirement of library personnel depends basically on job requirements in a particular library. The higher level personnel are responsible for the activities of the first stage as well as for the supervision, monitoring and evaluation of the activities of next lower level personnel in the hierarchical order. At every level there are the activities of supervision and control, solution of problems, reallocating duties, if any, so that the completion of jobs is ensured at every level. Different kinds of jobs and various types of activities in a library are neither of identical nature nor of same magnitude. There are activities of high academic and professional order involving highly technical expertise, activities of planning organising and management, as well as there are routine and repetitive jobs of various grades. The total workload for the present and the planned workload for the future should be taken into consideration to assess the requirement of library personnel at various levels A well-articulated organisational chart would help the management in this respect.

The total workload should be divided in two broad

categories such as, management and operational. At the middle level these two categories of activities may be overlapping. However, the specific job analysis and job descriptions can define the tasks of individuals in a definite manner. The number of persons required at different levels can be determined by analysis or the activities to be done by each individual at different levels on the basis of the total workload. For this reason, a well-defined and well-articulated hierarchy of operational activities must be prepared with the help of flowcharts for smooth operational activities assuring high standard of service.

JOB ANALYSIS

Job is a piece of work or may be pieces of work to be done by an individual, which while finished, lead to a result and become a part or activity. A job is the smallest unit of a planned network of activities. It is assigned to a particular person to be done within a stipulated time. Naturally, jobs should be carefully designed in order to get maximum organisational effectiveness. The library management is responsible to identify the task which should be included in the job. Jobs are the integral parts of a single function, process or activity. Therefore, the principle of job design should be closely related to perform the particular function, process or activity.

There are certain jobs which are fixed and also certain jobs which are dynamic. Some jobs should be done as a routine matter and repetitively and some jobs are performed by changed methods as required by the changing needs of the users as well as for use of technology in library activities. The management can get the idea and information regarding the tasks actually being done by an individual employee holding specific job only through the job analysis. In job analysis the assignment of responsibility is most important.

Every individual with a particular job or task is responsible to the next higher rank supervising the work. Job analysis may be illustrated in the following way showing the hierarchical order :

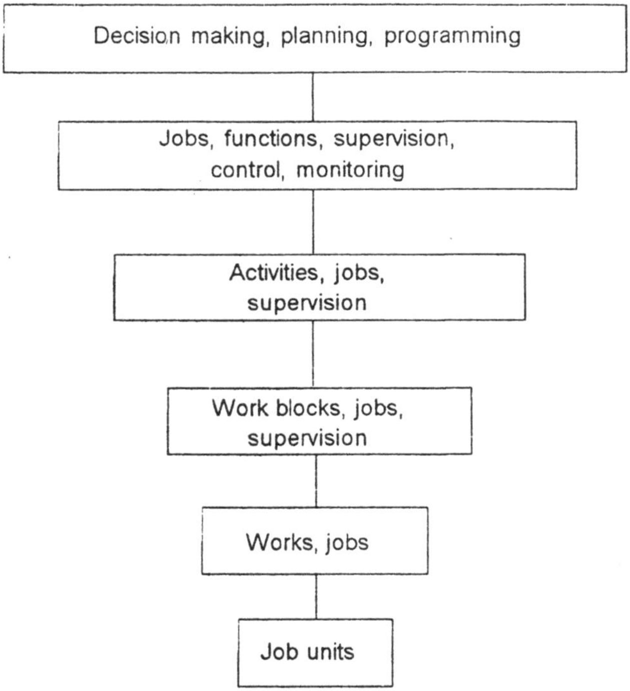

JOB ANALYSIS AT VARIOUS LEVELS

Jobs are done by every individual as assigned to him. The results of jobs may be tangible and intangible. At the operational level the result may be tangible but in the management level the results are intangible. Everything can be assessed by the effects of the result. The performance of every job can be done by an individual having good education, professional expertise, technical skill and adequate experience. All these should be considered in job analysis.

While the jobs, works, tasks and activities are analysed, they provide very important indicators to assess the entire operational process in the library. Job analysis helps to understand the step by step procedure of each operation, time required for each job, professional skill and experience needed for each job and the workflow in the library. If there is any bottleneck, it can be identified, located and rectified. It also helps to understand and fix up the academic qualifications, professional training and expertise for creation of the posts and selection of persons for appointment. It ensures performance ratings of the library personnel to use modern management techniques like time and motion study, programme, evaluation and review techniques (PERT) and operation research. Job description can be prepared by the analysis and staff manuals can be prepared to make the employees know their jobs and responsibilities. This is essential for computer application in library particularly for the preparation of work flow chart.

JOB DESCRIPTION

Job description should be a formal document in the library describing duties and responsibilities of the library personnel. The job description document establishes standards for accomplishing tasks, so it can serve as a performance evaluation tool. It also facilitates the job-audit process to evaluate the progress on regress of the library activities as a whole as well as it evaluate personal performance of individual employees. Each job or work unit should be identified and determined and the job description should be written. It will specify the task and duties associated with that particular job, the relationship of the job with other jobs in the units of the library and personal qualities required to perform the job such as, educational qualification, professional skill and experience. Specified job descriptions are very important for administration and personnel management. The management of the library may assess the prospective person for assignment. If required, proper orientation and training can be given to the person who has been newly appointed.

The job descriptions may vary from library to library considering the kind of the library, size of the library, number of users, nature of users services, total collection or holding in different physical format, methods followed in technical processing, circulation per day, users services rendered in the library, infrastructural facilities and resources of the library. Generally the following items should be incorporated in the job description record:

1. The job title.
2. The purpose of the job and its relation to other jobs in the unit.
3. Job activities and procedures including a description of the tasks to be performed and the time limit specified.
4. The duties and responsibilities of the incumbent with some flexibility, if required. The enumeration of tasks and procedures are very important part of the job description.
5. Title of the person to whom the incumbent will report after completion of the job or any problem relating to the job performance.
6. Salary scale of the incumbent.
7. Academic and professional qualifications required.
8. Experience or training required.

9. Promotion to next higher post.

10. Methods of performance rating.

SELECTION*

The library is an organised environment created for the activities to be performed in an atmosphere of cooperation and dynamic interaction. The library personnel are reliant upon each other for activities done by the individuals as well as for activities performed for the organisation as a whole to achieve the goals of the library. Human relationship is an important factor in any organisation. All the organisations are short of resources at any point of time both for maintenance and developmental work. Even if resources are there, all kinds of resources accumulated cannot be effective if human resource is not properly planned, designed, well-organised and motivated for the jobs to be performed and targets to be reached within the time schedule. The work situation in the library depends very much on the nature of the work to be performed, the procedures adopted, the policy framework chosen, principles agreed, structure of organisation determined, code of conduct followed and working environment motivated.

Therefore, the suitability of the individual in the particular library for the immediate post and for promotion thereafter as well as the attitude of the person to adjust with the work environment of the library is very important. In any library their is a number of personnel of various categories, which constitute the basic workforce. Selection of persons as new entrants is crucially important for two basic reasons. First, the person has to perform some jobs and has to be assigned certain responsibilities for the time being and for the future in various capacities. Secondly, the person has to accept the work environment with all motivation and must have psychological attachment to the library. The sense of belonging, motivation and identity with the library can be beneficial both to the individual and the library. In selecting a new candidate to a vacant post, both task abilities and social abilities should be considered.

In selection of candidates for recruitment usually two kinds of requirements are considered. The essential or basic qualifications, usually academic qualifications, professional qualifications and working experience for some period. For a particular position all the applicants possess the essential qualification. Therefore, more emphasis must be given on desirable qualifications which may be of various sorts according to the requirement of a particular library. The work environment, job description, expertise required, experience to perform some specific jobs, etc. may differ from library to library. The management of a library has to choose the particular person most suitable for the vacant position.

The key predictor of the candidate's ability to fit into the particular working environment is the interview method. It is possible to examine the academic background, knowledge of the subjects, general awareness, professional skill, area of expertise, personality, aptitude, leadership, general understanding, intelligence, knowledge of modern technological development, latest trends of the profession within the country and abroad and other qualities. The interview board can also assess the personal relation style, motivation, attitude, mode of thinking, ability to adjust with change, awareness in technological advancement, sense of cooperation, capability to accept challenges and efficiency of the candidates.

There may be two kinds of posts in the library, the

existing posts, now vacant for retirement on resignation, and the new posts created for specific job requirements. All the formalities must be completed for the creation of the new post before the publication of the advertisement asking applications for appointment. The advertisement should contain job specification, position and responsibilities, work environment and personality along with basic qualifications required. The new posts must be justified by workload and demand of the library. The librarian must consult the competent authority regarding scale of pay, position, job descriptions, essential and desirable qualifications. All the requirements should be reflected in the advertisement for appointment.

Selection of a candidate refers to the process of actually choosing the individual who will be capable to perform successfully in a job. The basic goal of selection is to achieve a good fit between the qualifications of the applicant and the requirement to the position. The successful matching of an applicant to a position is crucial because a wrong person will be a liability not only for himself but to the organisation as a whole for a long time. If the right person is not selected, the result will be:

1. Wastage of resources of the organisaiton,
2. Decreasing in the quality of service to users,
3. Wastage of man-hour and non-performance of jobs,
4. Reducing staff morale,
5. Wastage of time and energy of the supervision,
6. Activities of the library not done to the expectation,
7. Disruption of work environment.

The right person will be really the human resource. The person must have appropriate knowledge, professional skill, expertise and capability to perform the assignments from time to time. In addition to these, some characteristics are expected while in the work situation. These are :

1. Ability to communicate to share ideas,
2. Commitment to organisation with a sense of belonging,
3. Sincerity in purpose and action to be responsible and dedicated to work,
4. Attitude to grow and develop intellectually and organisationally,
5. Sense of cooperation to work with others having positive attitude to coworkers,
6. Creativity in thinking and activities to solve problems and to devise new solution,
7. Seriousness with desire to work hard to achieve the goals of the organisation,
8. Capability to accomplish the tasks assigned to and to adapt changes in the work environment.
9. Maturity having relevant experience to take right decisions, to face new situations and to explore new work environment.

INDUCTION AND ORIENTATION

When the persons are appointed to the particular posts and they join, the most important job of the management is to make arrangement for induction and orientation. The newly appointed persons are not expected to perform the jobs with much efficiency. They must get acclimatized to new work environment of the library. The induction and orientation programmes make the newly appointed persons confident in their work, motivate them to serve in the best way, inspire them to be involved in participating attitude and create a sense of belonging to the library and the parent organisation. The induction and orientation programmes are meant for any person at any level while appointed to the new position.

The programme should be designed to provide information in general about the library and the parent institution, the objectives, goals, functions and activities of the library. They should know the rules and regulations of the library and manner of working in the library. They should also know the organisational chart and hierarchical order of management, their respective duties and responsibilities and their specific roles in the work situations. The programmes should include the library's activities, services rendered, past achievements, relationships with other libraries and plans and programmes for future developments, and the like. They should make a tour to the library to be introduced with other library personnel and to be acquainted with the library procedures.

Orientation programme prepare the new employee a full and productive member of the organisation. Through orientation the employees get the focus to work environment and approach to job performance. They will be able to find how they fit into the total library structure. There is a difference between orientation and training. Training gives the employees such instructions and makes them acquainted with such techniques which will enable them to perform and complete the specific tasks of their jobs according to job specification and job description.

The orientation process is very important for the newly appointed employees for establishing and maintaining a positive and active attitude on the part of the employees. It is also important for making the employees enthusiastic to participate in all library activities and to accept the work environment as their own. The commitment of new employees to the organisation should be very high and they should be excited about coming to work. Orientation process inspire the employees to accept the challenge to work in various situations.

During the orientation process the new employees should get various printed materials, such as staff manual indicating rules and regulations of the library, organisational chart, description of different divisions and sections, work schedules, interrelationship of the departments and a total picture of the library. Orientation programmes should be conducted by senior persons to impart knowledge about the objectives and goals of the library and the parent organisation, work environment, activities, workflow, services rendered, assignments of the posts to which the persons are appointed and all relevant matters.

3

NEW LEADERSHIP : FISSION TO FUSION APPROACH

Leadership is most important in management and it has the vital role in human resource management. During the twentieth century there has been a sea-change in management principles and techniques. Managerial activities have been recognised as the guiding force of any organisation and, obviously, these activities depend on the leadership. The traditional management was, to a great extent, authoritarian and the approach was conservative. The librarian took all the decisions and issued the directions. All the works in the library were done under his guidance, supervision and control. The whole administration was based on individual's understanding, capability, far sight and judgement. The administrative procedures were unique and limited to individual libraries.

Henri Fayol, the founder of classical movement in management, formulated fourteen management principles. These are Division of work or specialisation, Authority and responsibility, Discipline, Unity of command, Unity of direction, Subordination of individual interest to general interest, Remuneration, Centralisation, Scalar chain or lines of command, Order, Equity, Stability of tenure of personnel, Initiative and Esprit de corps or a sense of belonging to the organisation and a corporate sense over self. He looked at administration from the top down through a "pyramid of control". L. Gulick and Lyndall Urwick followed Fayol's principles and gave emphasis on seven key principles. These are Planning, Organising, Staffing, Directing, Coordinating, Reporting and Budgeting. These headings denote seven kinds of functions of the head of the office or organisation. Their principles also follow the top to down administration.

Frederick Winslow Taylor propagated the scientific management school. His attitude towards management was that man and machine are similar. According to him these two elements work together and "it is no single element, but rather this whole combination, that constitutes scientific management, which may be summarized as: Science, not rule of thumb; harmony, not discord; Co operation, not individualism; Maximum output, in place of restricted output; the Development of each man to his greatest efficiency and prosperity". Taylor accepted many of his concepts from the bureaucratic model developed by Max Weber, particularly in regards to rules and procedures for the conduct of work in organisation. Max Weber, a behavioural scientist, first articulated a theory of authority structure in organisations and he distinguished between power and authority, between compelling action and voluntary response. He identified three characteristics which aided authority. These, in his opinion, are charisma on personality, tradition or custom, and bureaucracy structured and rigid rules and regulations.

The concept of bureaucracy developed about the same time as scientific management. Max Weber inspired the thoughts on specialisation of work, levels of authority and control of organisational activities. Weber was more concerned with the structure of the organisation in which people perform their work roles, rather than with the individual. He laid importance on specialisation of workforce, regulations to be adhered to, and procedures leading to the advantages of a hierarchical system in making informed decisions in an organisation. Weber stated that "experience tends universally to show that the purely bureaucratic type of administrative organisation ..... is, from a pure theoretical point of view, capable of attaining the highest degree of efficiency and is in this sense formally the most rational known means of carrying out imperative control over human beings." But Weber recognised the dangers of too rigid bureaucratic control at a later period and he stated, "a passion for bureaucracy is enough to drive one to despair."

During last half of the twentieth century almost all the organisations were guided by the management theories of Fayol and Taylor. No doubt, these theories founded the basics of the organisational structure of industries and other establishments and guided the systems of management. Till now, many organisations, including libraries depend very much on these classical and scientific theories as bases of their formal organisations. But gradually it has been found that these management principles have given undue emphasis on the formal aspects of organisational structure and management policy and, thus, neglected the human resource. The individual personality, potentiality of individuals, informal group interactions, intrapersonal communication, shared decision-making and such other human factors have not been taken into consideration.

Within such framework of management system, however small, attention was given to the personal attributes of the individuals working in organisations. Personnel factor became an important factor in work situations and persons working as a small group or as a large group were considered as work force. Personnel administration became an integral part of the management. Interpersonal relationship, staff participation and mutual cooperation were given prominence. Individuals were not just considered as work units but as human beings with human mind and feelings. The idea was that if the personal needs of the individuals are satisfied, their suggestions and complaints are considered and individuals feel a sense of belonging to the organisation, their morale would increase and it would enhance the production or output.

Several studies were undertaken and some concepts emerged on human relations approach and human behaviour trends. Emphasis was given on individual attitude and behaviour and the informal group in formal organisational structure. The studies demonstrated that workers are motivated by financial incentives, that workers are influenced by the group in their acts, that if the organisation makes employees happy, it will gain their full cooperation and optimum efficiency.

In an organisation people can be motivated by material inducements, desirable physical conditions of work, ideal benefactions, such as personal power, prestige, distinction, and the like.

The most widely acclaimed management theory is "Management by Objectives (MbO). It acts as behavioral guides for individuals and groups within the organisations. This technique has been used to merge individual goals with those of the organisation. It emphasises a combination of individual and organisational goal setting for the decision-making. This technique is most effective in industry and commerce or any profit-making organisation but it is being used in library situation because of its behavioral factors. Peter F. Drucker first defined the technique as ".... the setting of individual objectives pursuant to the organisational goals" in relation to the individual in an organisation. At the same time Drucker cautioned that this technique means the ability to direct oneself and one's work on the one hand, it can also mean domination of one person by another. He states that, "Objectives are the basis of "control" in the first sense; but they must never become the basis of "control" in the second, for this would defeat their purpose. Indeed, one of the major contributions of management by objectives is that it enables us to substitute management by self-control for management by domination."

Management by objectives is an example of participative management because it involves everyone in the management process to some extent. It clarifies responsibilities, strengthen planning and control and establish better relationships between managers and other staff members. In this technique the individuals have specific responsibilities, freedom to act, clear communication, shared responsibilities, personal accountability and improved personal capability.

Leadership is the prime factor in the management of any organisation. Leadership is responsible for decision-making, planning, organising, implementation, assessment and end-result. For obvious reasons leadership involves authority and power. It is a fact that authority and power to its full extent is vested at the top of the hierarchy in the library. Directions, orders and instructions are issued from top of the hierarchy and these are implemented by the respective levels of subordinates. The modern concept of management gives emphasis on the system of participation based, on a model of distributed power and mutually shared control having an involvement with all the affairs of the library. The higher and middle level persons having the authority and power vested in them attempt to guide and persuade and seek the suggestion and participation from the respective subordinates. Organising and performance of all the library activities are done with the active participation and support by involving the total workforce at various levels as an organic whole.

There are various theories in the area of human resource management. Personal quality theory has been emphasised in trait theories in which leader is accepted as the superior and the subordinates are expected to follow him by virtue of his personal qualities. In environmental theories the leadership is based on providing solutions in a given crisis. The leader may not be successful in a different situation. Personal-environmental theories give emphasis on personal characteristics, capability of managing various situations and response of subordinates to accept the leadership. Group interaction and its results are the focal concept of exchange theories.

Humanistic theories give emphasis on the leadership of persons who will grant maximum freedom to enable group members to achieve high level of self-actualisation having total involvement in all affairs leading to success. Expectational theories are based on leadership to be gained by a person who is able to maintain the aims and goals as well to motivate the group. According to Contingency theory no fixed pattern of leader behaviour can be effective in all situations. In a particular situation the leader must design his own pattern to achieve the best results. The contingent factors are the personality of the leader, personality of the group following, nature and complexity of the task involved, time schedule, availability of adequate resources and many other variables of a wide range depending on the situation. The successful leader must be person-oriented and task-oriented and should be capable of understanding the particular situation.

The leadership has to create a framework of activities, maintain norm and policies, motivate fellow members of the groups and allow others to prove their efficiency. In the complex social situation, while there are changing conditions under external influences, no one pattern of behaviour and approach is equally effective in all circumstances. R.M. Slogdill has the opinion that, "the task of a leader is indeed complex and attended by numerous conflicting demands, arising from differences in follower personality, ability and value commitment, changes in task requirements and changes that impinge upon the group." The leaders should be aware of changes in the wider environment and in the internal structure of the organisation. They should act effectively considering the situation keeping in mind the performances of every individual within a group and the achievements of the goals.

In a particular situation the leadership has to take the right decision for organising and implementation of a task. In the decision-making process staff participation is a major factor to obtain efficiency and ensure high performance. Staff participation can contribute to improved decision-making if the skill, expertise, knowledge and creativity of the staff members are utilised properly. In decision-making process there are a number of variables, such as attitude of the leadership, the behaviour style, involvement of the authority, extent of participation of the library personnel, quality of communication among the staff members, motivation of individuals and other related factors. John Cowley has mentioned the model of decision-making having five points. These are:

"1. **Own decision without detailed explanation**- in this instance the manager acts alone without reference to colleagues and without making any attempt to explain his decision;

2. **Own decision with detailed explanation** - here the manager decides on a course of action and gives reasons later;

3. **Prior consultation with subordinates** - discussion of the problem during which subordinates after their views and opinions; the manager then decides on a course of action which may or may not take into account advice offered;

4. **Joint decision-making with subordinates** - the manager and other workers on the problem together and reach a joint decision; here the participation is genuine and persons other than the manager will contribute substantially to the choice of a solution;

5. **Delegation of decision to subordinates** - where the manager hands over a problem to a member of the team; although the decision may be reported back, the manager will have little influence in the matter."

These five alternatives practically cover a wide range of managerial behaviour which may be used in different times under various circumstances. All these methods may be used in a variant way in a variant degree as a situation demands. Delegation of power is also an important element in personnel management if the person is suitable, efficient and expert. In the complex organisational system of a library where activities are performed in a flow chart model the top-down method is imperative to some extent. The concept of authority in the organisation is evident in organisational charts, administrative structure, job descriptions and system approach. But the situations are not against staff participation. The top-down structure can cooperate with bottom-up concept, and when both the ends meet at a point, the goal can be achieved.

FISSION APPROACH

An overview of a concept, theories, principles and techniques of administration and management discussed above show that management is an integral part of human society for organised efforts and organisations in particular. Management is required in organisations for production. The prime force of production is human endeavour. In any organisation the human factor is most crucial and, therefore, systematic approach to management was conceived. It was first legalistic with centralised power and authority, which was unquestionable. Then came the principles of classical and scientific management. While the organisations became very large and more complex, the human relations approach became vital. But all these theories and principles of management, more or less, assume that the authority, power, planning, decision making and developmental activities are vested in the top. All these percolate to the down at various levels in hierarchical order. There may be consultation, discussion, taking suggestions at the bottom but these are not mandatory to respective higher levels.

In all the organisations the participation and partnership of all the persons at all levels are not considered as equal. The position, status, office held, remuneration, administrative power, etc. at the particular point of hierarchical order determine the value of the person in the organisation, whatever may be the personal qualities of the person. Persons become the tools to perform assigned jobs and they are evaluated by the jobs 'given' to them. Human potentialities, attributes, qualities and discrete personality are ignored within the organisation where structure is more important than human qualities.

All the management principles and techniques applied to modern organisation are based on top-to-down theory, more or less, however compromising, fluid and participatory it may be. This top-to-down approach of human resource management has been considered as 'fission approach', which means separation or splitting apart. The term has been taken from nuclear physics. The fission energy comes from splitting apart the nucleus of atom, which requires levels of control system. The existing management techniques imply division of labour, distinctly separated roles of individuals, authoritative decision, boundaries encircling individuals, departmentalisation, erosion of interpersonal relationship, distracted motivation, and such other conditions which separate individuals and split the minds. Positions and roles separate the individuals. Team spirit, creativity, emotional attachment and cooperation are restricted to words only.

It is also fact that the fission approach management has been accepted all over the world in all types of organisations; industrial, production-oriented, financial, commercial where production output and net profit are the goals to achieve. But in non-profit organisation where social responsibilities and obligations are of prime importance, the vital factors should be mind, attitude, motivation, sense of belonging, sincerity of purpose and actions, vision, integrity, personal commitment and emotional attachment. These factors are important in 'fusion approach', particularly in human resource management.

FUSION APPROACH

As opposed to fission approach 'fusion approach', a term taken from nuclear physics means joining together. Fusion approach in management indicates active participation of human elements, not machine or other inanimate objects. This approach brings individuals together, makes bridge between human minds and achieve mutual goals by sharing personal vision and values. This approach of management is not authoritative, traditional and hierarchical. The levels of position, status, remuneration, office, etc. are immaterial, the prime objective is to achieve the goal of the organisation through personal ingenuity, integrity, sincerity of purpose, cooperation and exchange of ideas and sharing the wisdom for collective decision. The people do not work for the roles assigned to them only or perform the tasks in terms of money and material benefits. They become involved with heart and soul. Fusion approach is the new management paradigm in which the individuals and organisations can grow together. It can imbibe subtle forces of mind which can basically transform organisations beyond hierarchical framework of impersonal models.

In the present human management situation there are usually three management levels. Each level may have a number of layers. The three levels are top, middle and bottom levels. The top level is responsible for decision-making and its implementation. They may feel that they are only people who face the complex challenges both external and internal. The middle level people may feel they are controlled and unappreciated by the upper level management as well as not getting adequate response from the bottom level. Bottom level people may think they are oppressed to some extent and their problems are not being felt by the upper levels, and more important, their talents and sincerity of understanding to improve things are ignored. If such situation happens, no organisation can improve and work efficiently. The organisational change may occur if the human resource change their mindset.

The improvement, efficiency and effective job performance are possible by changing initiative, greater involvement and expression of individual creativity. Individual attributes and qualities can motivate other individuals towards better organisational change. Fusion approach depends on the mental forces and attitude to share the responsibilities of the organisation. The conceptual foundation of fusion approach for human resource management in organisations through mental attributes was introduced by Margaret Wheatley, Myron Kellner-Rogers, Ralph D. Stacey. It is observed by Richard L. Daft and Robert H. Lengel in *Fusion Leadership* that "When that happens, people self-organise, changing themselves and their systems to keep up with changing environments. Change then occurs without either top-down force or bottom-up resistance."

They further elaborate the idea as "Our understanding of change is based on a broader perspective of what people bring to the organisation. We show how to develop personal forces that make every person a leader – someone who will initiate change and take responsibility for its implementation. When large number of employees are thus empowered, they create a firestorm of improvement that sweeps away resistance." Such resistance may be organisational, interpersonal, status consciousness, egoistic, conventionalism, political, personal envy, conservativeness or of any kind.

Fusion approach reduces barriers by emphasising conversation, joint responsibility and information sharing. It implies a sense of unity among colleagues, perception of the organisational goals as a whole and feeling similarities rather than differences based on the sense of community in vision, norm, achieving goals by sharing partnership.

Cooperation, consensus, delegation of power, team work are concepts in existing management principles but these do not mean the fusion approach because the identity of personal ego is not annihilated and individuals maintain personal autonomy, individual separateness and idiosyncrasies of personal traits. Therefore, common interest is not served properly within organisational ambience. Fusion approach is based on subtle mental forces from within individuals which go beyond the self and embrace the organisation as an integrated whole. These mental forces are not tangible and hard to find. These imply vision, morale, passion, ingenuity, attachment to the organisation and corporate culture.

Mental forces are not only the subtle forces, information is also a subtle force. Daft and Lengel observe, 'Information, so abundant in today's word, is a subtle force. The meaning of information exists within people and is exchanged among people, but cannot be quantified, seen or tasted. Information reaching Eastern Europe was as responsible as the West's military might for the fall of the Berlin Wall and the Iron Certain." Subtle mental forces of individuals like the emotional, intellectual and spiritual abilities and understanding of situations are united and drawn together to achieve the goals of an organisation, the effect will be really great. They have explained it very aptly. In their words "Just as the capacity of a computer system is geometrically increased when computers are networked together, the brain, heart, and soul capacity of the organisation can be increased geometrically through fusion-based teamwork, dialogue, and the sharing of information."

Daft and Lengel identify six subtle forces of mind of an individual. The individual potentiality and ingenuity has been grouped in three categories. These are intellect, emotion and spirit. The subtle forces of intellect are mindfulness and vision. The subtle forces of emotion are heart and communication. The subtle forces of spirit are courage and integrity. These subtle forces signify the fusion approach of leadership. They have explained in the following way;

"Mindfulness includes independent thinking, personal creativity, an open mind that welcomes novel and unusual ideas, and thinking outside the box".

Vision is the higher purpose toward which people work that provides meaning and inspiration for their collaborative efforts.

Heart represents caring and compassion, the positive feelings and emotions that underlie connections and relationships in the workplace.

Communication is the act of symbolically influencing others with respect to vision, values, and emotions. Subtle communication also involves listening and discernment.

Courage is the motivation to step outside the traditional boundary and comfort zone, to take risks, to take the lead, to be a nonconformist, to stand up for something, and to be willing to make mistakes as a way to learn and grow.

Integrity is honesty, trust, and service to others, which means going beyond "me, me, me" to give something to the team and the organisation.

Fusion approach signifies joining together, establishing mutual relationships, absence of boundaries, human and organisational, sharing of information and responsibilities, interacting each other, exchange of vision, keeping the values, wholeness of purpose, and adaptability of situation and cooperation among all the persons. It does not mean top-to-bottom concept or bottom-to-top concept. Every one should be in his own place for the time being but every one is involved everywhere with one motivation, achieving the goals of the organisation. While computers are used in the libraries and the workforce is adapted to electronic environment, the work situation becomes changed and the conventional fission approach does not yield desired result. Supervision, control, hierarchical order of administration does not work because the work situation becomes professional and technological, everyone is interconnected to every one and the responsibilities are shared. A lacuna at a particular point can jeopardize the whole system. The leadership with fusion approach can achieve the goals of the library and fulfil the objectives.

4

MOTIVATION : HUMAN FACTORS

The vital factor in human resource management is the motivation of the workforce. Human resource is the essential and most important resource in the library. If the library personnel are rightly motivated, adequately qualified, sincere in their work, serious to achieve the result-oriented targets and sincerely feel a sense of belonging to the organisation, they can be regarded as the best resource of the library in comparison to all other physical resources. Only the human resource can overcome the constraints and limitations of other physical resources. For these reasons the selection and appointment of the library personnel should be in accordance with the jobs and responsibilities required in the library. The right person should be in the right position for the right job. The persons must have the expertise to perform the jobs. They should also be trained properly for the situations as and when required.

Supervisors at all levels are interested in motivation because it finally results the employee performance as well as organisational effectiveness. Supervisors can be able to motivate by providing an environment which induces workers to contribute to achieve the goals of the organisation.

The behavioural pattern of an individual can best be understood by observing his motivation. It has been experienced that most people do not work to the fullest extent of their capabilities and that most jobs do not require that they do so. Motivation can be defined as a willingness to utilise the full energy to achieve a goal and to perform a job successfully. Motivation is thus a process of mental attitude to understand rightly the job and to perform it yielding result in least possible time frame. The attitude of motivation varies from individual to individual and even in the same person changes over time and environment. Motivation of an individual is influenced by a number of both internal and external forces as well as psychological and environmental factors.

The most complex area of managing libraries is dealing with the workforce that affect job performance. Each individual is different by nature and characteristics, and each job entails its own tasks and work environment. Supervisors may also react differently in case of individuals. The task of supervisor is very hard. Supervisors have to motivate the subordinates, to get high performance and to lead the team work, sometimes with heterogeneous group of persons. At the same time they are very much responsible to the superiors for the output of their units or sections. The low output of any unit can affect the performance of the library as an organisation. The human resource can be utilised properly and objectives of the library can be fulfiled if there is a synchronisation of the three elements : human motivation, job satisfaction and commitment. More or less the ideal situation does not prevail in the libraries but attempt must be made.

A library system must have a well-defined, well structured and realistic manpower policy considering both the routine jobs and developmental programmes at the planning and management level. The organisational design and staff structure should facilitate the understanding of the role of individual, responsibilities to be discharged, adequate communication and group involvement in the system. All the members of the library staff must be kept informed of factors affecting their work and they should be given opportunities to make useful contribution to the general functioning of the library.

Well designed and effective manpower policy is a vital factor in the library system. It should consider both the existing staff as well as new persons to be recruited. This should be decided at the planning level and organisational level.

Every library is a division of the parent organisation. The organisational structure of the parent organisation, the financial stability of that organisation, rules, regulations and administrative procedures of the parent body must have the impact over the library. The objectives and goals of the parent organisation as well as the procedures for implementation may change from time to time. The library cannot be insular to such changes, rather the library must act as a supporting organ to the parent organisation. The personnel management of the parent body must have the impact over the same in the library. While planning the human resource management in the library such situations have to be considered carefully.

Another situation should be considered in human resource management and manpower planning in the library. All the organisations are constantly subject to change as social forces, external forces and new technology have their influence on individuals as well as organisations. No system or organisational structure is static. Therefore, emphasis should be given on changing situations, revised objectives and programme adjustments. The traditional hierarchical structure, organisational charts, authority and control and strict divisions of functions within the existing system cannot function effectively in a changed situation. The attitude of the library personnel should be flexible and responsive to the mode of operation with necessary job adjustments. They should not work in the routine manner without considering the performance of the library as a whole. In the library situation it is the service which matters and this service is not in one's own job but in the service of the library as a whole to fulfil the objectives and to achieve the goals. Therefore, the motivation of the library personnel is of prime importance. Every library staff must have the motivation without which the library cannot function. In selection of library personnel for recruitment the motivation factor must be an important one.

PARTICIPATIVE MANAGEMENT

In participative management the rank and file library staff are involved by having a chance to participate in the operation and governance of the library and in this way better decisions are made with staff involved and it leads to increased job satisfaction for all the library personnel. Participative management has the virtue of forcing decision making "down to the level best suited to it by virtue of the availability of relevant information and the effect of the decision on the operation." Because of the changing pattern of library service shared decision making has its own advantages. Participation by employees is more likely to increase commitment and satisfaction with the end-product.

The motivation factors can be improved through better organisation of work. The planning and implementation of work schedules in a better way, monitoring of the works done, elimination of bottle-necks in work schedules, proper flowcharting, assigning responsibilities to individuals, placing of right persons at right positions capable of performing the jobs, are the certain situations which influence the motivation factors. But highly effective factor is the participation of the staff. All it means the active cooperation between the management staff and the hierarchical subordinate staff at every level in the setting up and implementation of job-oriented objectives.

Planning and decision-making of long-term objectives of the library are to be determined at the top level of management. While these are established as the umbrella pattern, the medium-term objectives and the short-term implementation targets are to be set. The implementation and improvement targets must come from the staff themselves. Participation does not mean essentially the consultation with immediate subordinate persons or the instruction given from the immediate higher rank. Such consultation is motivational only when the higher rank takes the right decision and gets it accepted by the group working under him. In such situation the subordinate does not take the responsibility for the consequences and may become frustrated as he does not exercise personal responsibility although consultation is involved. Staff participation means the real commitment involved in every bit of work to be done by everybody and the responsibility for the consequences is shared by everybody in the system. The management must come first with the commitment because the authority lies with the management.

CHARACTERISTICS OF MOTIVATION

Motivation is an impulse innate or created, to work hard to achieve the goal by performing the assigned job.

It is distinguished from job satisfaction in the sense that job satisfaction involved an emotional evaluation of the employee himself. Satisfaction is measured whether the employees like or dislike their jobs for some reason. But motivation involves the employees' desire to do something and the attitude to achieve the goal by performing the duties sincerely. Motivation is a mental attitude which cannot be measured. But there are several characteristics that motivated workers demonstrate when they work.

Characteristics of motivation has been described by Martin L. Machr and Larry A. Braskamp in "Motivation Factor : A Theory of Personal Investment (1986) in the following way."

1. Direction

Employees are motivated to do many things; motivation can to some extent, be assessed by what choices employees make. If an employee chooses librarianship over teaching, then it is likely the individual has a stronger motivation to do library work. If an employee chooses to stand at the water cooler rather than work at the reference desk, then the lack of motivation for library work is similarly evident.

2. Persistence

A motivated worker will spend more time on a task than one with less motivation. In library work it is easy to find examples of the highly motivated, persistent librarian. One need only think of the reference librarian who, in response to a reference question, may spend hours seeking the answer.

3. Continuing Motivation

A motivated worker will return to a task even after

interruptions. Children's librarians often demonstrate continuing motivation. These highly motivated professionals, even after a full day's work, spend their evenings making additional preparations. Such examples are also common among library managers and directors whose dedication often exceeds the normal bounds of the workday.

4. Intensity

Motivated workers are more likely to work intensely; their concentration will be focused, less subject to distraction, and their energies will be specifically directed to the job tasks. Such workers may appear constantly busy.

5. Performance

There are, of course, other reasons why an employee performs well even when motivation is not present. But good performance may also be an exhibition of high motivation. An employee who is directed toward work, persistent, intense, and willing to work during nonwork hours is more likely to be a good performer.

Goal-based motivation can be accomplished through goal-setting. Motivation increases if specific, challenging, and difficult goals are established for employees. Those, who perform repetitive tasks, are better in performing goal-based motivation work, even with hard goals. It has been found that employees who were given specific goals that challenged their ability, performed better than those were given vague goals, such as 'do your best'. As a characteristic of motivation the right goal is critical. The goal must be difficult, but it must also be perceived as attainable by the employee. In case of difficult goals, it must be clear to the employee so that he knows exactly what is expected. It is important that a goal must be measurable so that its attainment can be easily ascertained by the employee. When the employee realises that the goal has been met, it provides needed feeling of accomplishment and this encourages further motivation.

Another characteristic of motivation is commitment. If on the part of employee commitment is not present, motivation cannot be high. The employees must be committed to a particular institution with the feeling of a sense of belonging to that institution. This emotional attachment enhances motivation. The organisational structure must be designed to strengthen the bonds with good and motivated workers. If the employees feel attached to the goals of the institution and identify themselves with these goals motivation will be increased.

FACTORS OF MOTIVATION

The factors of motivation depend on both personality traits and situations within the organisation. The individual personality traits are level of intelligence and ability, possession of necessary information for job performance, motivation level, self-confidence, attitude to cooperate with the co-workers, sincerity of purpose and sense of responsibility. The organisational aspects are budget support, tools and equipment available, congenial work situation, favourable environmental condition, good understanding among persons working at various level, well-planned flowcharts, material and moral support, and the like in work situations. Appreciation of good performance and target achievement by superiors is also an important factor.

There are two basic factors for motivation and for increasing the motivation of library personnel. One is human performance factor attributed to personality and genetic factor and the other is the environmental factor. Personality factor signifies certain personality traits consistently associated with high level of performance. These are intellectual ability, problem-solving skill, socio-economic status, educational level, career aspirations and leadership capabilities. These are genetic factors and personality characteristics that are formed in early life. These are evident in the stability of employee's attitude over time while in the same job, changed job or change of professional positions. Motivation of such personalities can be enhanced to get substantially and consistently increased employee's work productivity by guidance and training. Even less productive employees with such personality traits can perform jobs more efficiently. When people are being selected for any position in the library emphasis must be given to persons who are forceful, dynamic and creative.

The environmental factor signifies that the attitude and performance depend on environmental condition of the library and its work situations. To avail of the best performance from the employees the library must create a congenial environment, if required, by changing work situations, tasks and jobs, rearranging position description. The situational factors do play a substantial role in job performance. In order to get the maximum productivity from the library personnel, it is vital that supervisors at all levels must understand basic psychological and sociological needs of the employees. If the concept of employee's satisfaction, motivation, commitment and personality traits are understood, it is possible to identify and design those aspects of work situations that will have positive effects on job performance.

These two factors are closely associated and intermingled in the work situation. A person performs the job independently as an individual and at the same time he is an integral part of the total operational system where all the library personnel are involved. The motivation factor is not just the mental state of an individual to perform the duties described in job description, but it is much more complex. It very much concerns not only the tasks of an individual but the social and physical environment in which these tasks are performed. Therefore, in the broader perspective the job description and performance relate to a composite affair of the individuals, environment and motivation to work. The following conditions apply for appropriate performance :

1. The tasks of the specific job.
2. Relations with co-workers.
3. Relations with supervisors.
4. Relations with subordinates.
5. Organisational factors, such as salary, benefits, opportunity for promotion, contribution in decision making.
6. Relationship with broader professional and social values.

There are some variables in the motivation factors in case of individuals arising from personality traits, interaction with others, work situations and management policy of the library. These are :

1. The tasks of the job description.
2. Achievement in completing jobs successfully.
3. Recognition for the achievements.
4. The level of responsibility entructed.

5. Reward, tangible or intangible.
6. Promotion opportunities.
7. Training and education to enrich professional growth.
8. Interpersonal relationships with co-workers, superiors and subordinates.
9. Proficiency and skill of supervisors to guide and direct in the proper way.
10. Qualitative growth of the library as an organisation.

WORK ENVIRONMENT

The three concepts of motivation, job commitment and job satisfaction play a vital role in the total performance of an organisation, particularly in the library which is the service-oriented organisation. These three concepts are very closely related and the library management should design the workplace to get the best result from the workforce. An important approach of human resource management is job redesign. Job redesign presupposes that the job assignment must provide three basic needs of the employee. These are :

1. The need to have meaningful job description.
2. The need to feel responsible for the accomplishment of job assigned.
3. The need to get feedback regarding the job performed.

Meaningfulness of the job indicates the job assignment given to a person can be performed best by that person with best of his knowledge, skill and talent. The fulfilment of the targets will have great impact over the people and the organisation. Responsibility on the part of the employee indicates the way the jobs will be performed and designed by the employee and he will schedule the methods and control the related activities and will finally complete the job assignment. Feedback is the related information after completion of the job to the employee by the supervisor regarding the impact of the result of the job and an assessment by the concerned persons.

A job can be redesigned in two ways, horizontally and vertically. Horizontal redesigning involves job enlargement by increasing the number and variety of tasks related to achieve the target. Vertical redesigning involves job enrichment by increasing the participation of the employees in control and management activities so that they could have control over the area of work and they feel that it is not just a routine job but indicate their involvement. Through work redesigning the employees feel a sense of responsibility and psychological involvement leading to achievement after completion of the jobs.

The management approach of redesigning work schedules may be creating small units of workforce responsible for certain specific job requirements under the charge of a leader. After performance of the jobs written reports may be submitted to superior authority and other departments concerned to increase levels of recognition and awareness of the performance. In case of computer application the redesigned tasks may be assigned to such units requiring specialisation, so the employees can acquire expertise. Computer application, network services, communication technologies and information services are essential in library situations. All these will change the entire work situation, job description and performance targets. The library personnel must develop special expertise in various technologies, service patterns and management procedures.

Work environment can be enriched by in-service training, new education, short-term courses to learn and operate new technologies by which the library personnel can acquire updated knowledge and can grow professionally. Library management should create such supportive environment by providing opportunities to increase expertise, new area of knowledge and information, new types of job performance, self-confidence, leadership qualities and to accept challenging targets.

Work environment can be redesigned for increased productivity through staff development. It is similar to training and some of the characteristics are almost identical. Staff development differs from training in the sense that it does not have to deal with specific tasks of the job description. It involves developing the employees understanding of themselves and the library so that they can be better employees regardless to their specific positions. Staff development is an essential tool for increasing motivation and perceived by both employees and management at all levels as a meaningful and useful process. Staff development meets the requirements to attain the professional goals of the library personnel.

Staff development is essentially required in libraries because there is a need to prepare employees for future supervisory and management positions. It is also essential where the work environment is changing for the introduction of technological innovations. The library must determine what organisational needs can be met by staff development programmes. Staff development opportunities are more important for designing persons as reward and appreciation as well as to sustain motivation. Opportunities should be given to employees who have proved their worth to attend workshops, seminars and conferences to be acquainted with latest developments and new areas of knowledge and technical expertise.

There are several ways to design staff development programmes. Any one of these or all of these may be followed in libraries as and when required. These programmes should be held on periodical basis.

Committee work

The library management should attempt to develop employees by creating a number of internal committees for various purposes and selected staff may be appointed as members of such committees. It will help the staff members to broaden the perception regarding library management to understand the problems encountered, to get the idea of solving such problems and to develop skill. It will also be helpful for interpersonal communication, data collection for specific purposes, programme planning, decision making and report writing. It is vital to motivate employees for collective performance and to understand the real work situations.

In-house workshop

As and when required workshops should be organised on specific areas of operations, for example, user's services, classification and cataloguing, information storage, retrieval and transfer, preservation of library materials, and the like. External experts can be invited on specific areas for discussions, problem solving, guidance, technical knowledge, professional expertise, etc. The library personnel, in this way can have exposure to wider work situations.

Continuing education

Continuing educational programmes can be organised at various levels, for specific purposes, in-house or outside the library. Such programmes will strengthen weak areas of job performance, application of new methods, updating professional knowledge and enhancing technical skill.

Participation in conferences

Top level management and senior level supervisors can be sent to symposia, seminars and conferences of academic and professional bodies at national and international level. These are the gatherings of top level experts in their own fields, who can contribute and guide in gaining professional and academic knowledge. Such participation helps exchange of opinions and ideas, knowing the library situations within the country and outside the country, problems faced or solutions available and interactive communication.

Work environment can be more purposeful and meaningful and the workforce can be more productive by taking several steps to encourage involvement and participation. Library personnel should know that they are performing important and meaningful jobs. They are accomplishing the goals of the library as well as the parent institution. The sense of value and identity with the institution have impact over organisational performance. Job description should be made challenging and enriching. Focus should be on responding to employees achievements, sense of responsibility, sincerity, recognition and professional growth. This will increase job satisfaction, commitment, motivation and performance level. Management should arrange good orientation, in-service training and staff development programmes, opportunities for employees to demostrate commitment should be given properly.

THEORIES OF MOTIVATION

There are a number of theories on human motivation

in general. These cañ be applied for the personnel management in libraries also. Douglas Mc Gregor in his 'The human side of enterprise' (1960) describes that there are two contrasting sets of assumptions about individuals and their perceptions of work. According to him the Theory X assumes that the human being on an overage has an inherent dislike of work and always will avoid it. So, the personnel should be directed, controlled and even threatened, where necessary, to put them to work. They need directions for what to do and reluctant to take much responsibility in their work. They are also not ambitious and prefer to have a secure and predictable work situation. In contrast to this he describes the Theory Y which argues that motivation comes from within and one can work efficiently without persuation. He states –

1. Individual will seek responsibility when conditions are favourable to work.
2. Workers wish to develop and control their own commitments in a favourable work situation.
3. They will exercise self-direction and self control in the service of objectives to which they are committed under proper conditions.
4. They will learn to accept responsibility as well as they will seek it.
5. Workers will seek recognition for their achievements.
6. They will make significant contribution to achieve the goals of the organisation.

In a library situation both the theory X and Theory Y are applicable. Though the latter is optimistic. Motivation factors can be able to stimulate both the groups.

David C. McClelland in 'The Achieving Society' (1961)

developed the Achievement-Motivation Theory. In this theory he emphasised the importance of high levels of accomplishment or the satisfaction of 'achievement needs'. Though monetary reward, status and power have impact over the motivation of individual, he points out that the accomplishment of objectives is a prime factor. According to him individuals have a sense of achieving and will accept responsibility for problem-solving even in a adverse situation. The entrepreneurial activity within a controlled environment is liked by the individuals. If they are given the opportunity to develop in such situation they will prove their efficiency.

In the opinion of McClelland, the good manager is an individual who give subordinates their own feeling of responsibility and who organises and rewards subordinates in such a way that they can perform better. Such managers want the power to influence others; their effectiveness are based on building team spirit and commitment to organisational goals, not on a dictatorial approach.

The implications of McClalland's study for library managers are significant. Different types of individuals are required for different positions. Individuals motivated by achievement may be best at jobs that require clear tasks and goals, where autonomy, recognition, and challenge can be provided.

F. Herzberg in 'Work and the Nature of Man' (1968) described his Motivation-Hygine theory. He made an extensive examination of job satisfactions and dissatisfactions among various classes of professional and non-professional staff. He found that the causes of satisfaction were not the same as the causes of dissatisfaction. The factors providing satisfaction in a job situation are the 'motivating factors' and when these are absent in a situation the dissatisfaction causes in form of indifference. The elements of work generating positive feelings leading to greater productivity and job satisfaction are described as satisfiers. The elements having the reverse effects are described as dissatisfiers. The satisfiers are achievement, recognition, work itself, responsibility and advancement. These elements create a good climate of productivity and motivate individuals. On the other hand faulty planning, poor organisational policies, bad administration, environment lacking inspiration and motivation, non-recognition of achievements, and the like create dissatisfiers leading to low motivation and indifference.

The implications of this theory are that if an organisation wants to motivate its employees, it must focus on those factors that produce satisfaction, i.e. motivators, rather than emphasise aspects that produce dissatisfaction i.e. hygine factors. The job descriptions of the employees should be enriched by increasing opportunities to work with few controls, by exercising greater responsibility and authority, by encouraging the developing mastery over one's work, and by providing increasingly difficult and challenging tasks and responsibilities. The complexities of human motivation and the variety of factors that affect work attitudes have been highlighted in this theory.

The American psychologist, Abraham Maslow in his work 'Motivation and Personality' (1970) developed the theory that an individual is motivated by two kinds of needs - basic needs and those that are socially determined and that both of these must be satisfied to allow emotional maturity. The needs of an individual are in hierarchical order just like a pyramid. At the base, the lowest strata are the basic physiological needs for survival. Next higher are the safety needs concerned with physical and psychological well-being and next higher is the social well-being in terms of belonging and acceptance. Next higher to that are esteem needs and the selfconfidence derived from recognition and status. At the top is self-actualization - the zenith of the individual's needs whereby his own potentialities are realised fully. Maslow gave emphasis on the progressive nature of needs achievement. When the lowest level is satisfied the individual strives for the next higher and in this way he aspires for the zenith. According to him the progressive higher order should be created for the individuals in any work situation to get the best performance from the individuals. According to Maslow management should provide good salary for basic needs, then should provide safe and secure work situation. Attempts to stimulate motivation through other means without satisfying the basic needs lead to failure. Gradually the individuals should attain the top of pyramid, self-actualization.

SUBTLE FORCES OF MIND : WHEN MIND BLOSSOMS

In work situation certain objective systems are there in any organisation in human resource management. These tangible things are organisational charts, control system, work flow, job description, performance strategy, incentive programmes, supervision and control methods and the like. These are the external forces thrust upon the employees to make them work. In all the personnel management systems these forces are used more or less to control the mind of the employees and to motivate them. But these systems overlook the resource of the heart that exists within individuals. Supervisors and the management systems assume we-they mentality, an artificial barrier in between supervisor and subordinate at all levels. By this feeling both the parties can never touch the heart of the other and keep themselves separated from each other. Real motivation occurs when supervisors fuse with other levels not only in mind, in heart also.

In human resource management when subtle forces of mind come to surface, the people do work with heart with continually created self-motivation. In such situation there will be no top-down force or bottom-up resistance. Such attitude brings a broader perspective by developing personal forces that make every person a leader in his own sphere and this empowerment leads the organisation to achieve its goals. It creates ingenuity, creativity and organisational inertia.

The subtle forces of mind are invisible and always are kept beneath the surface. These are strongly felt by listening for unexpressed employee issues, a vision that binds people together, courage to stand alone and take independent action. Subtle forces are independent thinking, creativity and power to foresee the future. Subtle forces encourage people to act from inner knowing and from rational analysis and to believe in the potentiality of human beings. Daft and Lengel observes "The motivating power of personal subtle forces is that people yearn to use them, to be free to express more of their personal creativity, purpose, risk-taking instincts, and enthusiasm. Subtle forces are like the water contained in a reservoir that is pulled toward the ocean when the dam breaks, or like the oil waiting to escape in a gusher when the drill bit reaches deep enough. The yearning is within you and others, even if not obvious to the eye. Fusion leaders look beyond the easy-to-see physical and material world of rules, procedures, measurement, and direct supervision and appreciate people's yearning to express their essence as human beings."

The human body is a physical entity which is visible and tangible as well as is the container and the expresser of more subtle qualities. Subtle forces have no relationship with the body, they are in the mind, heart, and spirit within the body.

5

COMMUNICATION

Communication has a crucial role in human resource management. The communication must be clear as to the main purpose of the message, well-designed and self-explanatory. The content, purpose, areas of priority, activities involved and time schedule must be properly transmitted to the receiving end. The proper timing of the message is also important. Premature communication is often misunderstood or may be kept aside and finally forgotten. Delayed communication may cause ineffectiveness, failure of the purpose, activities not required, inaction and wastage of time and resources. There should be a design for the communicating methods based on earlier discussions or instructions given. Adequate attention should be given on sensitive view points, mutual trust and shared responsibility. Open consultation and jointly taken decisions make the concerned persons involved having their responsibilities and their respective commitment.

The persons who are in the management of the library are responsible for decision making, planning and organisation of the library followed by the activities for achieving goals. The activities of the library as a whole and the activities in the departments and sections of the library having their coordination as an organic system very much depend on the clear understanding of the ideas, methods of implementation of such ideas, request, instructions and directions of the management by the subordinates at every level. If the ideas are sound, decisions are result-oriented, methods of implementation are clearly understood and the job responsibilities are properly assigned to individuals and groups, then the activities of the library are performed properly. The success depends on communication in both the ways, top-down and bottom-up, and the transmission of directions from the management.

Communication may be in the form of discussion, oral instructions, written notes or advice on particular assignment in a work situation. But communication on all allied and related matters must be correlated having interrelationship with past, present and future activities. In course of decision making staff meetings play an very important role. The minutes of staff meetings must be kept in writing and sent to the persons concerned in the departments. Otherwise, this may lead to inaction, confusion and forgetfulness. Everybody should participate actively in the staff meetings to understand the significance of any direction on instruction to make it clear if there is any confusion and appraise the members regarding the situations anticipated to arise in future for taking any action. If the members are inattentive in staff meetings, their recollections may be faulty or impressionistic. On the other hand, if the written communications are not read carefully, these may be lost in files and ignored. The result is simply inaction.

The prime factor of good communication between supervisor and employee is understanding each other so that the objectives and goals of the organisation will be achieved. Management must establish effective and meaningful communication with the employees of all levels and categories to train, motivate and direct them, and for this purpose information and knowledge must be transmitted for the job at hand. Communication must be at the top of the list of organisational priorities. The capability of face to face communication will greatly help supervisory effectiveness.

STEPS IN THE COMMUNICATION PROCESS

There are a number of communication models developed in past few decades. These vary in certain respects but these include certain steps, which are the components of communication process. These are :

Source

Source is the sender of the message or the one who is giving the message. The source has certain thought, need, or information to communicate. He has primary responsibility for the beginning of the communication. He transmits the message.

Message

Message is the vital component, delivered in clear and concise language in some form that can be understood by both sender and receiver.

Channel

Whatever may be the form, the channel is link between the source and the receiver. The message is transmitted over the channel, which can be in any form. In face to face communication, the five senses especially the eyes and ears are the best communication channels. The written communication channel may be a letter, a note, a direction or instruction, a circular, etc. Remote verbal instruction may be on telephone or voice mail. Electronic communication may be e-mail, bulletin board, video display unit both for in-house and the remote interactive communication.

Receiver

Receiver is the person on the opposite end of the source who is the recipient of the message and who has to act on the basis of the message. The receiver must understand clearly the message itself without any confusion or doubt. In case of such condition he has to verify and ensure the content of the message with clear instructions.

Noise

Noise is neither a step or a component, but it often happens that hinders communication in the proper way between the source and the receiver. Noise may occur in the source at the time of transmission, in the message itself when not clearly stated, in the channel when it is not working in good condition, by the receiver when he cannot understand clearly the message with proper instruction.

Feedback

The last component is the feedback in the communication process during which the source and the receiver resolve any confusion, doubt or misunderstanding. Feedback is most important factor in any kind of communication, whenever required. It is a response to the original message to allow the source to know whether properly transmitted and understood. Two-way communication is most effective because the source is in direct communication with the receiver, but in one-way communication the source has no way of knowing whether the message was received and understood without feedback. Feedback is the only way to overcome the hindrances of communication.

METHODS OF COMMUNICATION

There is a variety of methods to communicate with the supervisors and subordinates. The best approach will depend upon the situation created for communication, time required for communication, the message itself and likelihood of success for a particular approach. Communication can be classified into three categories, written, oral and nonverbal. Each of these categories of communication plays a specific role in organisational communication and each has certain advantages and disadvantages associated with it. The three categories are given below :

Written Communication

It is the formal channel of communication. Managers write letters, directives, instructions, memos, reports, and the like. Written communication is the formal and lasting record and ensures uniformity in communicating individuals as well as groups. It has many problems which can create noise in communication if it is poorly written, does not define the scope of the problem, contains ambiguous instructions and with incomplete information.

Oral communication

It is conducted within individuals and groups. In oral communication there is opportunity for feedback through which clarification can be accomplished and noise can be minimised. It is a face-to-face communication and all participants can listen and give feedback until they reach mutual understanding. Communication can also be between individuals. Oral communication is the best way to resolve conflicting situations.

Non-Verbal Communication

It is any type of communication that is neither written nor spoken. Body language is a specific type of nonverbal communication. At the receiving end it may be observation, correlation of past events or incidents, feeling the attitude of individuals and groups. At the source end it may be behavioural pattern, showing neglect or attitude of welcome. Non-verval communication is vital to the process of communication and sometimes stronger than both written or oral communication.

Formal communication methods are notices, staff manuals, news letters, letters, memos, performance appraisal reports, organisational charts, annual reports, meeting reports, bulletin boards, etc. In some cases written communication methods can be an excellent follow-up to oral communication. Written communication must be in correct and clear language. Kathleen Moeller-Peiffer suggests the following points to remember to make written communication.

Organise your thoughts before you begin.

Consider the reading level of the receiver.

Include the 5 W's: who, what, when, where, and why.

Avoid negative statements.

Use a slightly formal style.

Write concisely.

Date your correspondence.

Send a copy to everyone mentioned in the document.

Always keep a copy for yourself.

Bulletin boards are good source of information to be communicated to everybody in the organisation. These are official information of any type. Information should be posted quickly as and when prepared. It is better to assign one employee to maintain the bulletin board with updated information. It can be used to inform as well as to educate. It should be placed near an area where the employees congregate. The area should be well-lighted and spacious.

Staff meetings are very important methods of communication with the employees of all levels. Meetings provide a face-to-face, formal communication process among supervisors and subordinates as well as among co-workers. But these meetings should be convened and organised by the management. Such meetings must be at regular intervals or whenever required and the decisions taken should be available to all the persons concerned. The decisions should be implemented within the stipulated period with sufficient feedback. After implementation, the results and problems, if any, should be reported to next meeting for adequate communication and understanding of the situations.

Through on-the-job counselling the supervisors can communicate with the subordinates when job-related guidance is required or problems occur. Such counselling can be a communication in a directive approach, in which question-and-answer structure may be used, or in a nondirective approach, in which subordinates are encouraged to do most of the talking. It may be regarding the problems faced, solutions suggested or better ways of performing jobs are discussed.

An informal communication channel is there in all the organisations which can be identified as rumours. It is caused because of false information, incomplete information, motivated and fabricated information, lack of communication, and such other reasons. Whenever it occurs the management or the supervisors should clarify the situation with correct information. Individuals or groups in the library must get the communication directly to eliminate ill feeling and misunderstanding among the staff members. It is possible through –

* Clarifying details of concerned misinformation.
* Relaying personal information in case of individuals.
* Explaining actual situation by the management.
* Providing feedback on employee's feelings.
* Facilitating employee interaction.

The supervisors must feed adequate information to avoid ill-feelings, misunderstanding. They must conteract negative thinking and prevent wasting time from listening to and repeating rumours. An environment should be created so that all the library personnel feel that they belong to the organisation.

FLOWS OF COMMUNICATION

Within an organisation communication essentially flow in three directions : downward, horizontally and upward. Downward communication means the communication which flows from superiors to subordinates. It is the most common type of communication within the organisation. Daniel Katz and Robert L. Kahn states five types of downward communication. These are :

1. Specific job directives (job instructions).
2. Information designed to produce understanding of the task and the relationship to other organisational tasks (job rationale).

3. Information about organizational procedures and practices.
4. Feedback to the subordinate about his performance, and
5. Information of an ideological character to inculcate a sense of mission (indoctrination of goals).

Library personnel at every level expect to receive necessary communication from the supervisors. There are some problems associated with downward communication. These are :

(a) Organisations often rely too much on written or mechanical methods, such as manuals, booklets, pamphlets, newsletters, notices, memorandum, directories, and the like for downward communication even when face-to-face communication and personal contact might be more effective.

(b) Organisations suffer from overload of messages. Easy copying facilities have made any number of copies of a document. Numerous letters, memos, instructions, announcements, etc. are being circulated which take more time to read and taking actions.

(c) The problem of filtering of information at the time of downward communication flow through several layers of hierarchical order in the organisation arises when messages are changed, shortened or lengthened. In such situations downward communication may not be that much effective.

Horizontal communication is the lateral exchange of information within an organisation. It is essential for task activities by individuals as well as by the members of an unit or section in the library. It may be necessary to make horizontal communication with individuals working in other units. At each management or supervisory level, when required, horizontal communication is essential. In a library all the activities are performed in a chain system. The timeliness and the accomplishment of the operational activities depend very much on the performance of activities of preceding unit or section. Horizontal communication fulfils the following purposes :

(a) information sharing

(b) experience sharing

(c) task coordination

(d) problem solving

(e) conflict resolution

Horizontal communication does not follow the chain of command but depends on cooperation, mutual understanding, attitude to help or advise others for the accomplishment of activities and an environment of achieving the goals of the library. For the success of horizontal communication the essential elements are personal relationships to encourage the job situation, cooperation by sharing jobs when necessary, knowledge of interdepartmental activities and ready response to the needs of activities in the complex and dynamic environment of the library.

Upward communication contains messages from subordinates to the supervisors or management. Messages are usually asking direction, questions, clarification, making suggestions and providing feedback. Upward communication plays a vital role in the effectiveness of any organisation. Through the messages communicated by subordinates supervisors at all levels and the management can get a clear picture of the activities and ongoing states of the activities. They can understand also the problems confronted by the subordinates at all levels. But upward communication can be effective and meaningful if the management personnel take a positive attitude and encourage it for the interest of the organisation. Supervisors at all levels should be open minded and psychologically free for best utilisation of upward communication. They should be sympathetic listeners and should encourage informal contacts with the subordinates at all levels. Whatever may be the position in the library anybody may have suggestions for better performance and work environment. There may be problems of doing the jobs, behavioural attitude, ideosyncracies, lack of cooperation and coordination or anything else. The management should be aware of such problems from time to time. Upward communication is the only method to know the situation at ground level.

In these three flows of information, it is better to conduct face-to-face communication in appropriate conditions. This facilitates immediate clarification of any misunderstanding and lack of understanding and both the parties become satisfied. The verbal communication skills can be improved by improving listening habits. Russell Drum states, "as long as we are human, we will continue to see things as we are instead of as they are." Supervisors must be empathetic if they are to hear the problems of their subordinates and suggestions by them. They should act upon them in an appropriate manner. Feedback is most important. Library staff should see actions and decisions resulting from their suggestions. If not accepted, the reasons for that should be communicated. It is to be remembered that the staff members are as interested in talking with the supervisors as the supervisors are with them. The people who really work take pride in their work, and they like to be told how they are doing. Everybody wants appreciation and encouragement. The staff members also like to know what is going on in the library. Supervisors want to know the interest of the subordinates. At the same time the subordinates want to know the interest of the supervisors.

BARRIERS TO COMMUNICATION

There are many barriers to communication. Barriers may be created at any point - source, message, channel and receiver. Noise makes interruption and distortion in the communication channel. Carl Rogers observes, "Words are poor conveyors of meaning; in fact, it is a wonder that two people ever do understand one another."

Oral communications may be forgotten, misunderstood or found confusing. These may not be taken with proper attention and sometimes these may be self-contradictory. Oral instructions may be sometimes distorted intentionally or unintentionally, may be taken reluctantly or without due importance. Therefore, oral communication having influence on future actions should be supported by written communications on record as far as practicable. Written communications have also many barriers. A written record may be badly worded, ambiguously written and wrongly distributed. The medium of communication may be wrongly chosen. Sometimes the instructions may be contradictory to the previous instructions given, if these are not made considering all the aspects of a situation.

Therefore, all the written instructions should be sent to all the individuals concerned and to all the departments or sections of the library dealing with the matter. But it is also a fact that the biggest barrier of communication may be the individual receiving the communication. The reception, perception and understanding of a message by the individual is very much related to his personality, experience, expertise, general intelligence and capability to tackle a situation. The personal understanding and bias of an individual with a particular view of things may influence the interpretation of a communication in a different way.

The complex organisation, as the library is, should be divided into divisions, departments, sections and units. Each such division must have its own identity as an organic part of the library as a whole. The interdepartmental communication and the intra-departmental communication must be organised and transmitted clearly, precisely and effectively. Recognising the barriers of communication the management staff must make attempt to communicate rightly and should monitor the actions of the communications as well as must get the feedback. In this way the gaps in communication can be identified and proper steps can be taken to overcome the situation.

Peter Drucker has made three observations on communication.

These are :

1. It is the recipient who communicates; the so-called communicator only utters.
2. People can only understand within the limits of their experience (a point long recognized by teachers of rhetoric, but forgotten again and again by practitioners of communication).
3. People, as a rule, perceive only what they expect to perceive.

The true nature and characteristics of communication

have been depicted in these observations. The problems of communication cannot be solved only by listening to others, either top-down or bottom-up. If the management staff cannot communicate downwards properly, it is very difficult for a subordinate to communicate upwards. Therefore, the management should have a dialogue on specific objectives and activities with the subordinates at respective levels regarding their contributions to be made. If both the parties do not agree, proper communication cannot lead to the decisions agreed by both the parties. The dialogue, participation, involvement and commitment on the part of everybody concerned can make the communication most effective and meaningful. The creation of communicative environment will encourage the staff.

Barriers to communication are evident in the following situations. The supervisors at all levels should be alert and they have to check and monitor such situations.

The employee performs the wrong task.

The employee fails to accept responsibility for his actions.

The employee does not recognise priorities.

The supervisor is not aware of problems until they are emergencies.

The attitude of the employee is vague, misses the point, changes the subject or says yes too often.

The employee is inattentive, reluctant and makes someone responsible for not doing the tasks.

The employee often finds some excuse for not doing the task.

The employee does not cooperate and finds faults with others.

EFFECTIVE COMMUNICATION

Effective communication can exist only in a condusive environment. If the relationship between the supervisor and the staff members is good and understanding is clear, satisfactory communication is possible. The sense of responsibility and motivation, sincerity and sense of belonging to the library create the environment of good communication. Effective and meaningful communication cannot exist in isolation or in one-way directives of the management. Supervisors and employees must strive for harmonious working relationships, based on mutual trust and understanding. Effective communication will result in higher employee morale, steady productivity and efficient work situation. It is the only way to fulfil the objectives and to achieve the goals of the library.

Generally communication works in various forms and in many situations. Not only the personal communication, but the organisational communication plays vital role. The divisions, departments, sections, units of a library are different entities for various kinds of activities, but these separate parts of the library are tied together with the only objective and purpose of achieving its goals. Since library is a service-based institution, human resource is the most powerful resource in the library. Communication is the multifaceted binding force within the institution.

Alex Bavels and Dermot Barrett observe "It is entirely possible to view an organisation as an elaborate system for gathering, evaluating, recombining, and disseminating information... Communication is not a secondary or derived aspect of an organisation - a "helper" of the other and presumably more basic functions. Rather, it is the essence of organized activity and the basic process out of which all other functions derive." Organisational communication has been defined by Gerald Goldhaber as "The process of creating and exchanging messages within a network of interdependent relationships to cope with environmental uncertainty.". All organisational communication shares certain common characteristics. It occurs within a complex structure of activities, which is influenced by and which has its impact over the organisational environment. On one hand, there are the components of communication, such as the steps, the methods, the flows of communication and on the other hand, there are the people, their motivation, attitude, feelings, relationships, capabilities, skills, performance and aspirations. The guiding and deciding forces are essentially the people involved in the library.

6

Training: Need And Implementation

Learning is essentially a continuing process for activities that are performed and skills that are used in library situation. Every day the people face situations for which they must be educated, trained, and oriented in order to manage the complex work situation. It is not sufficient to have knowledge, the skills should be acquired to enable the library staff to use the knowledge. It brings confidence in the ability to make judgements and control the environment in which people function. In modern times library and information profession is under continuous change, the changes in operational process and methods, changes in technology, changes in activities, changes in work environment, changes in users 'services, changes in needs and requirements of the users, and as a whole, changes in the concept of library and information services.

The relationship between trained and competent staff and quality service is apparent to the recipients of service in any organisation. It is also a fact that supervisors fail to realise that poor performance and inefficient service within their own departments may result from lack of training. The in-service job training is essential in libraries to enhance and maintain the service quality and to play the crucial role in the increasingly complex and competitive information society. The libraries are service organisation which are affected by the satisfaction that the users feel. The service level and the quality of support of the library should be to the optimum expectations of the user community. The library staff require adequate training so that they can handle more diverse and demanding assignments.

Library management must foresee the changing requirements of the user community. Library staff should be able to assess the needs of library users, predict directions, and identify new services as well as those that are not in much demand. Library staff should not wait for the user dissatisfaction, expressed or unexpressed. In that case the library will be seen as a passive and non-responsive organisation. The library staff should be prepared to respond effectively to the changing context of Library and information services while maintaining respect for traditional values of the organisation.

The computer and communication technologies and the new innovations in these areas have great impact over library environment and service patterns. Generation, storage, retrieval and dissemination of data in the electronic environment, commercialization of databases and their updatedness, CD-ROM and on-line access, global network of information services, library cooperation and resource sharing and library networkings all these situations have changed the library services. The traditional library services, both in concept and operational activities have become outdated and obsolete, particularly in information service areas. Services through electronic media have placed tremendous demand in the library situation, and the library personnel are in hardpressed condition to build electronic environment in the library. The condition of electronic library is not that much satisfactory because the technologies themselves are changing every time because of new innovation in the technological areas. From time to time adaptation to changed systems have become essential. All these situations have great impact over the library personnel.

Under such impending situations it is imperative that the library personnel at all levels require an impressive array of knowledge, skills and abilities to perform the library activities to fulfill the objectives. Library management and supervisors must organise the training understanding the long-term impact that training has on the individuals and on the library itself. Training must be periodical, but continuing according to the specific requirement at various levels. Training should be job or activity oriented for the operational systems. For any kind of new service to be introduced, new section to be opened training must be arranged. The individuals or groups already trained should be trained also for a new work situation. It will enhance the skills, capability and job performance. The goals of the library will be achieved by the motivation, dedication, quality, skills and expertise of the library personnel. Training plays a crucial role in ensuring that the library staff are preferred to take the responsibilities.

Training must be effective and meaningful for particular purpose and specific job requirement. In our country the human resource is under-used and the proper resource is unrealised for library effectiveness. In libraries a large number of work problems are there in performance, communication, motivation, attitude, morale, sincerity and taking responsibilities. A number of barriers prevent acceptable performance and contribute to poor work relationships because the persons are not properly trained psychologically and professionally for the responsibilities they have to discharge.

Even the enthusiastic, energetic and sincere library staff at the beginning of their service life become apathetic or disillusioned after some time because of the improper work environment and stagnant work condition of routine jobs. The serious and sincere workers get frustrated because no new horizons are at sight. Even if, trainings are organised, these are not properly guided and integrated for particular purpose, aimless and practically useless because of the lack of motivation. Such trainings are not activated in new job situation. The damaging consequences of poor job training become evident in the attitude of the library staff. It is a clear wastage of human resource.

TRAINING OBJECTIVE

The basic objective of training is to impart education and give practice to the group of library staff on a specific job area in order to bring to a desired standard of efficiency and skill. Training brings a change to betterment through increase in knowledge, the acquisition of necessary skill. development of confidence and good judgment. Training cannot be successful unless the trained persons can develop efficiency, demonstrate a new job performance and can behave in a different way better than before.

There are several dimensions in each job description which an employee must achieve through the training. The job performance must be better after each training programme. These are stated below.

MOTIVATION

Motivation is an attitude to get oneself involved on any job of activity assigned to a person. No doubt, this attitude is an attribute of n person which is inherent more or less. Training does not mean class room teaching. One should undergo training to do the job in a better way. But one cannot do the job better if he is not mentally involved and eager to do the job. This mental involvement with the job can be enhanced by training through encouragement, inspiration, competitive attitude and by unfolding one's self through exploration of potentialities unknown to him. Training process can motivate an employee by specification of jobs suitable to him.

Knowledge

Knowledge is the conceptual part of a subject and the theories on which the subject is based. It is also the understanding of a subject or branches of knowledge. It is the mass of information needed to perform job descriptions or a set a activities efficiently and effectively. Knowledge in essential to perform the activities.

Ability

Ability is the worthiness to perform any activity. It comes from knowledge, experience, command over the processes or method in doing the jobs. It is intangible quality and characteristics that are necessary for performance of particular activity. It refers to personal characteristics to work with group dynamics, sense of cooperation, attitude to service, leadership and personal quality to work within a group and make others to perform the jobs. It can be enhanced through training process.

Skill

Skill is the capability to perform the jobs in the best

way. It refers to knowledge of methods, techniques and experience to perform the jobs taking responsibility and providing results.

Expertise

Expertise is the highest skill to perform the jobs with full technical knowledge of specific job or area. It is a combination of knowledge, professional techniques, experience and technological know-how.

Training programmes should be structured to enhance the dimensions of job activities for the specific objectives and purpose. The participants in a training programme must be a homogeneous group having appropriate professional knowledge and skill. Training programme should provide both theoretical and practical aspects. The objectives and goals of the training programme should be clear enough to the participants so that they can understand what additional input they will get through the training as well as what outcome or result is desired from the participants. This will be revealed in the feedback of the participants of a particular training programme.

Generally training programmes are focused narrowly on providing instructions regarding specific library activities to enhance the performance standard. But the training programmes will not be successful if a broader context is not provided keeping in mind the goals of the organisation, and if the needs of the individual employee are ignored. Each training programme must be effective and meaningful both for the individual participants as well as for the organisation as a whole.

During the training period the supervisors and the faculty should give due emphasis on the concept of corporate culture, an important and well-known concept in business management, which is essential in any organisation. The sense and respect of corporate culture create the particular nature and character of the organisation and a sense of belonging to the organisation. Libraries are social setting consisting of the parent organisation, the library itself, the library personnel, the users of the library and all other persons and organisations associated with the library. A library is characterized by the human resource and the services they offer. Each library has specific requirements in the roles, responsibilities, behavioural patterns, communication media and goals to achieve.

Corporate culture awards the library its distinctive character. It becomes the identity of the library in the outer world. Miriam Drake identifies the corporate culture as representing a "set of values and beliefs shared by people working in an organisation. It represents employees' collective judgments about the future based on past corporate rewards and punishments, heroes, villains, myths, successes and failures". The individuals are very much concerned and become part and parcel of the corporate culture of the library and their identities are determined by the corporate culture they belong to. Drake observes that" understanding the corporate culture and acting in accordance with the culture often determines a person's success or failure on the job. A qualified and competent employee may fail because he or she does not fit in, while a less competent person who understands the culture has a higher probability of success".

All training programmes conducted in the library for all the levels of employees must contain the concept of corporate culture in the library. All the employee must learn and adapt to the corporate culture. Such learning will guide the employees how to behave in a particular environment, what formal and informal guidelines exist for acceptable behaviour, what should be the roles and relationship among personnel in the library and what are the values and philosophy to be owned by the individuals and groups. The understanding of such values makes the process of integrating people in the library.

The sense of corporate culture is particularly critical when technological change is introduced in the library. The magnitude of such change can cause a total disruption of the existing manual work environment habitual to all the people. Some may become apprehensive, some may become peaceful and some may not understand the potentialities of the technological changeover. If the required motivation and total involvement are not there, it will be difficult to make the implementation. The library management and supervisors need to identify the aims and characteristics of the library in such situation, and must educate the library personnel that existing manual methods are not consistent with long term objectives of the library and the changed electronic environment can serve to achieve the goals of the library in global communication network. Education, training and motivation can be used to adjust and strengthen the changeover process. The corporate culture of organisational identity, cooperation and collaboration can overcome the psychological practice and can establish a common ideal for the new environment.

EDUCATION FOR SENIOR POSITIONS

In modern libraries education and training cannot be limited to particular position, particular group and particular job description. According to the requirement of particular purpose education and training must be imparted to groups of persons at any level. It should be a continuing and ongoing process as and when the situation will demand. Persons in senior position are the leaders in own spheres and they not only work for individual jobs but they are also responsible to guide, direct, advise, counsel and manage other persons within their administrative areas. In general, they have the following responsibilities.

* Planning designing and implementation of strategies for library and information service with most convenient format to the clientele and end-users,
* Collection management and making the library holding a repository of significant resources, both for knowledge and information,
* Making balanced collection of print media, non-book media and electronic media,
* Management of human resource for optimum utilization of all other resources,
* Organising training programmes to enhance skills and expertise from time to time in accordance with the changing patterns of technology and the changing needs and requirements of the users.

Management and supervisory staff need continuing education which develop their cognitive skills and their managerial knowledge. The persons require the following attributes.

1. They must have the management skills with a vision to plan, control and monitor the jobs and activities, users services and personnel management. They are responsible for policy making building consensus for future visions of library operations and better users services. They should make planning, budgeting and implementation of the visions. Supervising the work

teams and their accomplishment to achieve unit objectives and institutional goals is an essential attribute.

2. They should be research-minded in academic areas to guide and give academic input to the users seeking such assistance. Orientation for technological, financial and operational research should be attributes for personal development.

3. Financial planning, control and budgeting for infrastructure facilities, resource allocation are essential attributes. Libraries have to operate under severe financial constraints for ever-increasing expenditure for collection development, administrative cost and users services. A good budget sense helps to make choice among various alternatives and to be economic.

4. Supervisors as the leaders need to be educated about the intellectual ordering of their work so that they can develop cognitive maps to anticipate users needs technological innovations, and explore avenues to serve the users in the best possible way. They should make the existing system most useful and efficient as well as foresee the future trends.

5. Supervisors and management staff must acquire continuing education for life long professional learning. Knowledge is ever-expanding and has become more specialised. The operational areas have become more complex. Continuing education is the most profound need in library education.

TRAINING FACTORS

The essential and most vital factor of training is the change and change in every respect. Training should result in some change as compared to pre-training condition. It should be demonstration of skill or some knowledge not previously held. Through the training process the employees can be prepared to operate successfully in the library environment over a long period time. Training should be given periodically to work in the library in all its departments and not only in a particular department. In that case the view will be narrow just to perform the job descriptions and activities with a narrow outlook. Training should create self-confidence, loyalty, motivation, skill, and a host of other positive attributes like sense of cooperation, collaboration, responsibility and overall ability to contribute and to adopt to future changes.

Training should reflect the reality of the library situation as a place in which change is constant and development is a continuous process. Basically the employees are trained in specific knowledge and skill but the sense of work value should be increased. Through the training process the library staff get the attribute in cultivating an attitude that will enable them to work effectively within a changing environment. Training typically focuses on building a commitment to the tasks at hand, learning them, and carrying them out in a directed way.

The changes in library situation, particularly when electronic environment has to be created, there may be some staff problems regarding lack of skill or ability to perform in the new environment or to accept the new system or method of work while accustomed in the existing methods of work. Some staff resist to change because they lack certain knowledge or skills or some staff may apprehend that they may lose control because of the rigidity of the system requirements or their work will be more closely monitored.

The most prevalent problem is attitude towards change. The sense of losing something of value with the change, such as experience in particular activities, methods of doing the jobs, skills in particular job requirements, recognition or status keeps people away from the change. The supervisors should feel and should have sympathy to persons with such attitude. The best approach to overcome such attitude is the training process, in which the supervisors and the faculty can explain the changing situation and work environment, and that the existing staff are the people who will initiate the change and who will work in the changed environment. The training process can educate the staff and prepare the staff to enhance capability, motivation, commitment, and challenging attitude to work. Training must focus on the person being trained as well as the activities to be performed. The management and the supervisors must be very sensitive to the needs of the trainee, his attitude, motivation, skill, knowledge, ability and understanding. If the training process is properly planned, designed, organised and conducted, it will not only strenghten the staff, but the library itself to achieve the goals.

A training programme is not just the training schedule to be operated during a specified period of time with a number of training sessions, theoretical and practical. Before making a training programme there must be idea about the purpose of the training on specific topic, how this particular training programme will contribute to the library requirements, area of training, duration of training, selection of faculty including concerned supervisors, selection of participants, production of course materials, feedback schedule, evaluation of the trainees, and such other related activities. The most important point is whether this training programme is essential, training time is accurate, participants are the right persons, and to what extent the training will benefit the library activities. There is no point to make the programmes for training's, sake. Each training programme is very expensive in terms of money, man-hour of faculty and trainees, organisational cost and management involvement.

Training programme is the primary responsibility of the supervisor concerned for developing his staff. This commitment to staff should include major attention to job training. The most important point is how effective a supervisor wishes the training to be. Training must not be a routine matter or procedural tasks to be performed or on adhoc in approach. A systematic approach to training, well-conceived and well-implemented training programme can produce the best result both for the employee as well as for the library.

The supervisor is the key person in human resource development. Unmotivated, poorly trained and inefficient staff are always a liability to the management. The knowledgeable and skilled, motivated and committed staff can only deliver the results. The supervisor working with his subordinates in a unit or section is directly involved in the basic activities can directly influence the working environment that affect staff attitudes towards job performance, towards co-workers, towards user community, towards the library, and ultimately towards themselves as members of the organisation. A well-planned and responsive training process can be an asset if the staff feel encouraged to participate in learning in an active way, to develop self-confidence, to educate themselves, to improve capability to succeed, to develop positive values towards their work, and to identify themselves with the library.

A supervisor has major impact and effect over the

efficiency of the unit operation and morale of the individual employees. Supervisors play the roles of both guide and leader. He provides direction, information and guidance to the staff. He also exercises the commitment to the overall development of the staff. He must have contribution to the growth and development of all the persons of his unit or section. Supervisors should recognise the dynamic and critical link between effective training and alround efficiency of the trainees. The efficiency earned by training is the contribution to the individual as well as to the organisation. Supervisors should review and evaluate the training programme to monitor the results.

After completion of the training schedule the supervisor should make review to determine the condition as observed by Sheila D. Creth as follows:

"A strong sense of support for the person to succeed.

A sense that the person has value to the organisation because of the importance of the work and of the person.

A recognition that the person has knowledge, skills, and abilities that are worthwhile to the library.

An understanding that the success of the person will contribute to the department and to the library.

A sense that as an individual, the person is a welcome addition to the staff."

The supervisor should recognise the learning process based on learning principles. By this way he can be more realistic in getting training result. Creth identifies the following learning principles particularly relevant to the training situation.

1. People learn when they are ready to learn.
2. Learning is an active not a passive function.
3. Learning occurs through trial and error.
4. Learning occurs through association.
5. Learning is multisensory.
6. People usually learn one thing at a time.
7. People must understand in order to learn.
8. Learning occurs from practice.
9. Positive feedback is necessary for learning.
10. Learning is unique to the individual.
11. Learning is affected by the order in which information is presented.
12. Rate of forgetting tends to be rapid immediately after learning.
13. Learning is increased if knowledge of results is understood.
14. Learning something new can interfere with remembering something learned earlier.

These learning principles should be remembered while planning, designing and selecting course content and course modules, preparing course schedules, allotting course hours for each course unit, keeping time for interaction and interpersonal communication. Feedback is a vital tool for reviewing the training activities.

PLANNING AND DESIGNING

Before making the planning for training the need for the particular training course should be ascertained as a part of the human resource development programme as a whole, the objectives of the training should be defined and the suitable period should be fixed. Obviously the faculty for the training course including the supervisors should be selected and the target group for whom the training course has to be organised should be selected. The planning for the training requires a commitment of time and effort form the supervisor as well as financial grant and available necessary infrastructural facilities from the library management. While the initial planning is completed, if required, it can be modified and updated. Any training programme can be repeated with necessary modification for another target group while found necessary. But there should be gradational relationships among the training courses and each training programme must be considered as a component of human resource development programme in the library on the whole.

Supervisors of respective sections or departments should act as the incharge of the training programmes for the workforce working with them. They understand their own people, their efficiency and deficiency as individuals as well as in groups. The supervisors are aware of the reasons for having difficulties in understanding certain concepts, procedures, workflow and techniques. The supervisors can make the training programmes having the total perspective in their mind. They should consider meticulously the needs of the individuals, target group as a whole, and the training required. Then the supervisors may be able to identify training methods, course content and learning process.

Training programmes are organised for a group of individuals having identical jobs and related jobs. According to the training objectives it may be departmental or forming a group with individuals working similar tasks in various departments or sections. The more vital factors of training are the training course objectives and components as well as the target group who will be selected for a training programme with some specific requirements. The first step of training is to identify the results which are specific for accomplishment of the tasks for which training programme is organised. The academic components of the training course should be designed to get the desired results.

The next step is the job analysis both for individual's job description as well as job description of a number of persons having identical nature. It is to be considered what benefit will be gained after the training programme. For this reason a detailed analysis should be made regarding work assignments, work flow, work procedures, and even specific activities and services. Job analysis should also be made for addressing performance problems and for implementation of a change in procedure or service. It is important to avoid the methods of activities repeating in the same way because these are being done, better methods should be thought of for improvement in job performance. Management must assure that the available human resources are being used for the most critical needs of the section or the department. The supervisor should review the work that needs to be accomplished according to units of job analysis.

Analysis of job tasks is essential to know the specific information about job content and job responsibilities for the identification of all job tasks, time for completion of individual tasks, critical tasks of the jobs as well as knowledge, skills and abilities needed to perform each task. Analysis of job task identifies both functional and specific job requirements. The functional job requirement means the unit of task performance as expected from an employee within a specified time limit. Specific skills, knowledge and abilities enable an employee to perform a task with specific procedure or technology. Job analysis indicates all pieces of tasks that make up the total job under consideration. The job analysis by tasks enables the supervisor to know the area of tasks, to provide detailed information about job requirements as well as about the tools and resources needed to perform each task. Such detailed job analysis prepares the supervisor to make changes in the job assigned as required and to take decision on the areas of job training.

All the units of job must be supervised and monitored following the job descriptions. The supervisor should see the activities of subordinates on task performance, tools required and time consumed. For this purpose a comprehensive list of job tasks should be compiled. Time schedules should be estimated for each job task. It may be daily on working day, weekly or monthly according the job requirements. The time estimate is important to know whether the tasks are performed in time or getting slow. The employees should know also what is expected from them.

There are a lot of jobs in the library which have the greatest impact on the department known as critical jobs. These types of jobs must be performed in scheduled time frame with required priorities. The recognition of critical tasks is the policy decision of management at any level, but the persons entrusted for such type of tasks must have clear understanding of performance expectations. The training programme should be focused to meet the required performance. The scales of priorities of job tasks should be clearly identified and should be made known to the employees concerned.

For performing the jobs the employees require knowledge, skills and ability. Knowledge means the clear understanding of the job performance with full information required. Skill indicates the capability to use the knowledge in performing tasks and ability is the self-confidence, attitude and commitment to make the jobs complete. The supervisor should know all these attributes of the employees working under his supervision and he should identify the weakness or limitations of individuals in work situations. These three attributes are overlapping and interrelated and cannot be separated objectively. But the supervisor can understand on the review of the job performance of the individuals. With this understanding the supervisor can design the training course components such as, content, focus and sequence for providing training to individuals. The course content should contain academic theories, practical training for proficiency in skill and motivation for involvement in task performance.

Training courses should be designed to keep the performance standard at the highest level. It means completion of a job within the schedule time frame most efficiently and with minimum error rate, if any. The supervisor should define performance expectations, so that the employees can strive for the performance the supervisor wants. If it is not defined individual employees may establish their own standards of performance, which will impare the library activities. But the employees who actually perform the job tasks may be asked to suggest their views on quality. The mutual development of performance expectations may help to attain good performance standard. The performance standards for the jobs, when established, should be included in the training course content. Obviously, the standard should be based on the performance of fully trained and knowledgeable staff.

TRAINING METHODS

While the training programme on a particular course content is designed, the methods of training are to be considered. The success of any training course depends practically on the training methods. There are various types of training methods depending on the course content, levels of participants, purpose of training and results to be achieved. Warren in his 'Training for Results' outlines the following criteria to consider in selecting a training method.

* Training criteria
* Trainee response and feedback
* Instructor skill level and feedback
* Approximation to the job
* Adaptability to trainee differences
* Cost.

The selection of training method should consider "How easily can the instruction be delivered in terms of logistical and scheduling problems?" The method should consider quality of instruction to be maintained using the particular method as well as whether the method is acceptable to the trainees. Two very important points have been raised by Sheila D. Creth as she observes, "Innovative methods for training should not exceed a department's ability to be successful in using them, nor should traditional approaches be relied on when they clearly do not meet the learning requirements of particular jobs or the needs of trainees."

Primarily, lecture and discussion method is valuable to provide the background information and ideas to the trainees. Academic input, regarding the course content is also essential. The supervisors should discuss organisational information, such as objective of the library and requirements of the department according to priorities. Motivation and performance expectations are important. The trainees should understand in advance regarding the content and focus of the discussion and expected result from the session. The method should follow structured discussion so that learning of the trainees can be evaluated on verbal responses. There should be adequate personal interaction between the trainer and the trainees. A clear understanding on both the sides must be there regarding objectives of the training programme and the desired result.

The demonstration method should be used for job training. In this method the trainer explains specific procedures, equipment, and task performance to the trainees by demonstrating how a task is performed, how to respond in a specific situation, and the like. It is a practical training method in which the trainer shows how the job has to be performed and then by the trainees to follow it. Evaluation of the trainees can be done readily. This method of training provides an useful way for observing, correcting, and supporting the trainees as they learn.

The training materials play an important role during training process. The formats and techniques that can be considered for use in developing training materials include written aids, such as programmed or self-instructional; audiovisual aids; such as slide, tape, transparencies, film strips; video cassettes; computer-assisted instruction like computer application for simulation training. The appropriate formats and techniques for training materials are determined by the course content and skills to be taught.

To make the training effective and meaningful, and to achieve the best results the role of interactive communication is both vital and crucial. There are specific communication needs that exist during the training process. The effective communication during the training period builds a positive foundation for future interactions and interpersonal relations with the trainees. The communication process may be formal or informal. But the employees should understand that the communication is not only for the training period but also for the real work situations continually in the organisational environment. Communication is an interactive, multi-dimensional act concerning interpersonal relationships.

During the training process and after the completion of the training course the trainees should make the feedback in both formal and informal way. The trainees' progress and understanding occur during the instruction process as the trainer observes responses and performance. Progress should be reviewed also periodically by the trainer through consultation with the trainees. It allows everyone involved in the training to review progress and problems, if any. While reviewing, it is essential to evaluate the progress of individual trainees. The constructive and continual feedback should be achieved by avoiding the barriers of effective feedback, which are either criticism and negative attitude or useless praise leading to no constructive results. Continual and constructive feedback contribute to an effective work environment in which learning and improvement represent a shared value. It can be achieved when the trainer share knowledge and information listening to the problem, gives instructions to support the needs and requirements of the trainees, invites communication from individual trainees, explains, demonstrates and feeds the problems of the individual. The trainer should make everybody involved and participative.

TRAINING EVALUATION

The purpose of training evaluation is to gather and analyse information in order to justify past actions and to project the future use of the human resource, in particular and other resources. The evaluation of each training course reveals its usefulness, effectiveness and limitations, if any. Each training course should be interrelated to the previously conducted courses as well as training courses to be planned and designed in future. Each course should make improvements in training for effective application in library operations and activities.

Barbara Conroy observes that the following goals can be achieved through the evaluation of training:

* Furnish accurate information to assist further planning, to improve decision-making and to document achievements.
* Determine to what extent program and/or activity is accomplishing its goals and objectives, and what results are being achieved.
* Identify program strengths and weaknesses and the reasons for specific successes and failures.
* Assure more consistent quality in learning activities and efforts.
* Reinforce learning and develop an awareness of growth and change.
* Determine the cost and benefits of the programme and its activities.
* Justify the investment and answer demands for accountability.
* Produce documentation that allows information to be shared with others.

These points can serve as a set of broad objectives for the evaluation of job training. As a matter or principle all job training courses should be evaluated, but there are differences in approach to evaluation and methodology based on the objectives and the target groups for whom the training is provided. The methodology of evaluation should vary for different training situations, different status of trainee groups and for specific training techniques with electronic tools. The general training programmes for subordinate employees and specific technological training for the supervisors must have differences in objectives, techniques, intensivenesss, technological expertise. Therefore, parameters for evaluation must differ.

The training supervisors, the trainers and the trainees all of them have crucial role in evaluation of training regarding content, methodology and results achieved . Everyone involved in the evaluation process should share a common goal. The supervisor has the responsibility to prepare the modalities how the evaluation will be accomplished and for analysing the results of training course in order to make future decisions. The observations and discussions with the faculty and staff involved in the training process can help the evaluation results. The supervisor can focus on the overall impact of training on departmental performance relating to work flow, improvement of services, motivation and interpersonal relationship among the staff members. The trainees are most concerned with every thing of the training course in its totality. They should be tuned to the learning environment, improving skills, developing motivation and collaboration.

In the evaluation of job training two aspects are most important, an assessment of the trainee's performance as the result of training, and the effectiveness and efficiency of the training. The performance of the trainee should be considered in the light of desired performance of the training itself. Evaluation of personal performance of the trainee depends on the desired change of behaviour, ability to perform the tasks and activities at a higher level and acquiring adequate knowledge and skill. The trainee has also a role in the process of evaluation. The trainee's reaction to training regarding the content, its appropriateness, methods, relationship among the topics and logical purpose of learning must be considered seriously. Job training evaluation is a very important source of information in considering ways to improve the use of most valuable resource, the human resource.

7

ORIENTATION : NEW EMPLOYEES

There is a basic difference between training and orientation. Training emplies giving teaching and practice to the employees in particular work situation and activities in library operations in order to bring to a desired standard of efficiency, behaviour and capacity with motivation and in collaboration with co-workers in library environment. Usually training is given to those who are already in library service and it is in-service training for improvement in job accomplishement and for development of individuals to serve the library in a meaningful way. Orientation is not the training in specific area of activities, but to make oneself familiar with the overall situation of the library as a new entrant and to acquaint oneself with the new organisation, new work environment and the people working in the library. Orientation is to make oneself familiar to stand within the surroundings of activities and people of an organisation.

The new employees are newly inducted in the library and their needs differ from the needs of existing employees because they are new. It does not matter in what position or level of the organisation one was working, or how much previous work experience one had before joining to the new organisation, it is the fact that the environment of the new organisation is new to the newly entrant. The new employee has to undergo a learning process not only related to policies, procedures and job duties, but he has to learn also about his role in the new organisation, the expected behaviours, the personnel, the work style and the culture of the organisation.

During the initial period of a new job, the individual operates to a large extent in a vacuum regarding interpersonal relationships and performance expectations as well as lacks the knowledge and skills needed to perform effectively in the new work situation. This situation generates some degree of anxiety and nervousness, and creates lack of confidence. One may feel alienated in such situation. This may be disruptive in job performance and in learning. The negative feelings impair both work situation and human relationship.

Therefore, new employees in an organisation must have positive feelings, which are curiosity, motivation, enthusiasm and a sense of challenge to show their worth. The supervisors in respective departments should establish an environment of positive feelings. Through the positive feelings the new employees can develop a sense of commitment to their work and willingness to show their ability. The supervisors and co-workers should have support, co-operation and sympathy to initiate in their jobs and should keep feel the new employees as in-siders. They should assure the new employees a comfortable working environment, meaningful working relationships among the co-workers and right communication. In this way the new employees can be absorbed in their respective positions in the new library situation. Initially this process is effective to some extent in the individual's own work environment so far individual's jobs are concerned. Unless the new employee knows the organisation as a whole, its aims and objectives, goals to achieve, style of functioning, service patterns, techniques followed, interpersonal relationships, job analysis and job descriptions, deployment of human resource, long-term, medium-term and short-term planning, organisational set up, technological capability, administrative set up and distribution of activities, infrastructural and other resources, responsibilities and obligations of total human resource, and the library as a whole, the new employees will not be able to function properly as an integral part of the library. Their motivation, capability, commitment and sense of belonging to the organisation can inspire them to contribute their best.

Orientation of the new employees in the library is the best way to absorb them in the main stream. Orientation should be fitted to the individual as much as possible to get the best out of oneself. But group orientation is also essential for general awareness and background information. The knowledge, skills and capability expected should be a part of group orientation. After joining, whether individual or group, the employees must be initiaed to the library's own workforce. The organised plan for orientation ensures increased morale and productivity.

JOINING THE LIBRARY

Orientation programme for the new employees is a formal educational aid and a kind of initial training. It is not held just on the day of joining of individual employee, but according to the orientation programme of the library. At the initial period the supervisor and the co-workers give a primary orientation. The joining day is crucial for the new employee and can have significant impact on reducing nervousness and encouraging a positive attitude. The new employee must submit the joining report and should be introduced to the supervisor and the co-workers. He should be given a general outline of the job description to be aware of the activities and responsiblities. He should know the working hours, duty chart, library rules and regulations. He should have a tour to the entire library building and various departments to know the work environment and the library staff.

Within a few days the new employee should understand the functions of other departments and how his department interacts with other departments. He should be familiar with the organisational chart and how the library is related to the parent organisation, its plans and goals. In the meantime he should know the history and philosophy of the library and the parent organisation. His knowledge of job description, duties and responsibilities, supervisor to report, co-workers to work with, operational processes, departmentalisation of the library, his position among co-workers - all these will enable him to be productive and acceptable to his co-workers.

NEED FOR ORIENTATION

Every library has its own nature and characteristics depending on the objectives and goals of the parent organisation. Moreover, each library differs from other libraries, even among the same kind of library because of size, infrastructural facilities, financial and other resources, technology adopted, working situation, long-term and short-term planning, library collection, categories of users and their specific needs and requirement, and the like. Therefore, the orientation programme of a library will be execlusive to the needs, workforce and suitability of that library.

Practically new employee orientation programme begins on the first day after joining by the supervisor and co-workers in an informal way. It is essential as observed by H. Lan Addams "Upto Speed in 90 days : An Orientation Plan" (1985). He states that "Employee performance is often directly related to attitude, and, therefore, shaping a positive attitude must begin on the first day of work and continue throughout the first few months." According to Claudia Reinhardt the formal new employee orientation programmes "reduce turnover and absenteeism, prevent performance problems, instill positive attitudes about the organization, and pave the way for better communication between the supervisor and the new employee."

The need for new employee orientation programme is universal in any kind of library. The immediate and long-term benefits of new employee orientation programme are obtained by the new employee as well as the library. The new employee develops self-confidence to serve the library with better performance. The library also gets the benefits in the long run due to enhanced employee job satisfaction and improved productivity. The objectives of the new employee orientation programme have been suggested by H. Scott Davis in the following way:

* To make all new library employees feel welcome and comfortable as they begin the new job;
* To provide consistent documentation and interpretation of major library policies and philosphies for all new employees and, in course of doing so, strive to avoid "information overload";
* To acquaint all new library employees with other library staff and other departments and units within the library system;

* To provide continuing orientation support to all new employees during the initial months of their employment through mentoring and other activities.
* To tailor individual orientation activities/information according to the varying information needs for different positions within the library and, in doing so, to be mindful of individual differences among new employees in terms of personal experience and educational background;
* To emphasize the new employee's role and potential for contributing to the overall mission of the unit/ department, division, and library; and, finally.
* To call attention to the importance of continuing staff development and the library's commitment to staff training, and to emphasize new employee's share of responsibility in self-initiating/communicating staff development needs to their supervisor.

ORIENTATION MATERIALS

Study materials have to be prepared for the orientation programme as well as skill and knowledge training. Supervisors need to identify orientation materials that are required for the new employees appointed in different departments and at various levels of service. Orientation materials are not of very high standard or not much technical in comparison to the training courses materials for in-service training. But the orientation materials for new systems or new programmes both for the new employees and existing employees should be technical in nature. Whatever may be the topics the orientation materials should be expressive, easy to learn, inspiring and well-documented. Orientation materials appropriate for new employees should include the following topics to give them a better perspective.

* The objectives, organisational structure, size, activities and other relevant information of the parent organisation and its relationship with the library.
* Description of the mission, goals, policies, procedures, services, and other information of the library.
* Library organisational chart, description of basic activities of the divisions and departments of the library.
* Organisational charts of the departments, description of activities performed by the departments, names and position of the library staff of the departments, location of the departments and workflow.
* Description of classification scheme followed, catalogue code used, charging system, and other technical works.
* Job description of individual new employee, names of immediate supervisor and co-workers.
* A short history of the library and its progress reports.

The purpose of the orientation is to provide a work context and one's position in the work situation in relation to co-workness. It will help the new employee to contribute the best performance, to get clear understanding about work environment and to have the commitment to work.

In addition to the preliminary orientation materials, instructional materials may be prepared in the library for effective training. Library operations are becoming complex, particularly with the use of automated systems. The new employee orientation should be limited to the state-of-the-art activities of the library, whether manual, automated or partially automated. Training programme should not be organised with indequate materials or nonexistent materials like computer. It will create confusion at the time of actual implementation of electronic environment. The changeover requires strategic, technological and communication support with a totally new training programme both for new employees and existing employees.

The preparation of training materials is a difficult job. It requires considerable skill and technical knowledge to produce quality materials needed. Training materials should be prepared for specific purpose with specific and sufficient information. A library manual cannot be used as training material. Orientation should be given to new employees on the activities and operations actually being done in the library.

Training materials should support the personal instruction given by supervisors. Personal interaction is the best method of communication which is to be supported by the training materials. Inter-personal communication is needed to clarify, to test knowledge and ability, as well as to support and encourage. In developing materials the following points should be considered.

1. Orientation materials should be designed to provide information on a single task or activity at a time,
2. The materials should improve the skill of the trainees,
3. New employees should be able to use the materials independently,
4. Training materials should be used for practical training during training sessions,
5. New employees should have the opportunities for self-testing so that they can make self-assessment about their skill and knowledge.

SUPERVISOR TRAINER

Initial orientation of the new employees and job-specific training are the responsibility of the immediate supervisor. Therefore, he should be actively involved in making a structured new employee orientation programme. It is assumed that all supervisors are equally competant in their jobs. They understand the value of a programme designed to provide complete and consistent information to the new employees.

The responsibilities of immediate supervisors for orientation of new employees are given below:

* New employee should be introduced to co-workers in his work area;
* The work space with furniture and tools should be arranged for the new employee;
* Library policies and regulations are to be explained relating to job performance;
* To accompany new employee to visit related sections and superior officers;
* Departmental procedure should be explained;
* Written job description, performance evalution criteria and job processes are to be discussed with documents;
* Personal contact should be made with the new employee whenever required for assistance, guidance and overall looking after;
* Any kind of problems faced by the new employee should be solved;
* Assisting in new employee orientation coordinator selection;

* Review of new employee orientation content with the coordinator;
* Preparation of new employee's workplace;
* Reviews with new employees regarding major library-wide policies and procedures, job descriptions and performance evaulation process;
* Maintaining new employee orientation checklist;
* Maintaining appropriate communication with new employee orientation coordinator;
* Participating in new employee orientation programme evaluation.

Responsibilities of the new employees are to be acquainted with library procedures, job descriptions and co-workers. At the time of orientation programme they should do the following :

* Review of new employee orientation programme materials;
* Ask questions and seek clarification as needed;
* Interact with immediate supervisor and new employee orientation coordinator;
* Participating in new employee orientation scheduled activities;
* Participating in new employee orientation programme evaluation.

There should be a close cooperation between supervisor, course coordinator and new employees and all the doubts should be clarified adequately.

ORIENTATION PROGRAMME

The orientation programme involves individualised

orientation activities conducted during a new employee's first few days on the job, and continuing, as needed, throughout the initial months of his employment. The appropriate orientation content for particular position should be determined by the immediate supervisor and the course coordinator prior to the joining date of a new employee. Each new employee should know the orientation programme in detail. The maximum orientation period may be three months of duration. But major activities of orientation should be during first few weeks. The activities may be semi-structured in that they require scheduling of one or more orientation sessions. Each session is flexible in terms of duration, content covered, and order of presentation.

An overall programme evaluation should be conducted at a logical frequency that allows enough time to collect sufficient data. During all phases of evaluating the programme, it should be emphasised that the purpose of the evaluation process is to evaluate the orientation programme, not the individuals involved in it. The best measure of an orientation programme's effectiveness lies in the input provided by the new employees who have gone through the programme. Informal input can be obtained through interpersonal interactions with course coordinator and supervisor.

8

Team Work : Participation and Collaboration

The fundamental unit of activities and operation in the modern organisation is the group and not the individual. In the rapidly changing work environment in the libraries, in which computer technologies, communication technologies, networking, global access and changing needs of the library users are creating tensions in all aspects of library operations and service patterns. The library professional need to be able to create new visions for information services and materialise these visions into meaningful services. Library professionals need to work together, within the individual organisation as well as like a group of professionals across the country for collaborative work groups to design new systems and services. Particularly decision making in this period of constant change, makes it imperative that library professionals develop their understanding of the process of communication and group decision making and develop their skill and expertise for working effectively in this new environment.

Planning, decision making and creating organisational

structure in the library are often complex, expensive and skill-based. The library professionals are required to communicate efficiently and creatively with ever-increasing satisfaction. All the activities can be efficiently performed through team work with the participation and collaboration of all the library personnel. A great deal of organisational communication accurs in meetings, formal or informal, convened for particular issues. As a part of organisational life the professionals can enhance their skill and understanding and select the process by which the library users can be served through quality ideas, decisions and expertise.

The library personnel must be capable for facing the challenges for reshaping library services in the context of innovation, productivity and competition. Because of the rapid change of using technologies and the increasing emphasis on productivity and innovation within the information service community, the library professionals have to be able to increase services for productivity and respond innovatively to the users needs and requirements while also reducing costs in all counts. These situations need to create a greater reliance on specific and quick communication and the creation of organisational structures and processes that are more participative and collaborative. The commitment of all the library personnel to change behaviour and service patterns can be achieved through participation and collaboration. The supervisors and subordinates at all levels need to understand both the mechanics of participation and the relationship aspects.

As a service organisation the library offers services and the service is the product of the library. Product is not always a tangible one. In modern times information is the power, product and resource. In all spheres of human activities right information and its timeliness is the most valuable resource. Such resource must be utilised for the benefit of the human society. Librarians act as information providers. This is the productivity of the library. In this age of competition libraries can survive with high productivity. Snyder and Edwards in their paper presented at the American Library Association annual general meeting in 1991 stated that "the only consistently effective means by which an individual or organization can improve productivity is to bring more and better information to bear on all types and levels of problem-solving, planning, designing and decision-making." For the purpose of improved productivity more personnel in an organisation need to be involved in contributing information for better productivity.

Rosabeth Moss Kanter observes that productivity is not just a "mechanical issue of input and output." Kanter states that the definition input output of productivity is the result of "the confusion of efficiency with effectiveness... And as Peter Drucker has long pointed out, efficiency is doing things right; effectiveness is doing the right things. And doing the wrong things less expensively is not much help." Kanter further states "Aspect of productivity that needs serious attention... is, rather, the capacity of the organisation to satisfy customer needs most fully with whatever resources it has at its disposal. This may require modification of product, development of entirely new products, or changes in the ways they are delivered... [This] calls out for innovation - indeed for innovative thinking on every level of the organization's affairs."

David Osborne observes that both public and private institutions "must be flexible, adaptable and innovative. They must search constantly for new ways to improve services and highten productivity." These two terms are correlated. Productivity improvement requires innovation and innovation improves productivity. As in other organisations, these two terms are crucial in library profession. Now information is the most vital product and commodity which must be marketed. Marketing of information has been an important part of library and information service during last decade. Before that libraries were the primary institutions to collect, organise and make available all kinds of information to all segments of society free of cost to the individual user. Such scenario has been changed radically. Many organiations and individuals offer what was previously known as library service. They serve with greater flexibility and timeliness. Now there are numerous commercial organisations owning updated large databases selling the information product available online globally. Many individuals and organisations are willing to pay adequate charges for such information products and services. Now it has become a very competitive market. Such situation was completely unknown to the library professionals before two decades but now it is a reality.

The electronic information packages, product variation, availability in different formats suitable to users needs, instantaneous online access to information, networked environment and such other facilities have made library service to some extent irrelevant except traditional services. Library and information services can be valued in a rapidly changing information society if new approaches to services and newly designed services are ensured. The electronic library environment requires the professionals who can make proper planning, take right decisions, contribute best ideas and can give leadership in all segments of library operations. The library must have a well-planned and properly designed organisational structure, best technological infrastructure and support, sophisticated technical processes and, above all, a team of motivated personnel prepared to accept new approaches, operational tools, electronic services, challenging job descriptions, time-bound job assignments and leading roles in electronic environment. The persons must have high academic and professional education, skills and expertise.

COLLABORATIVE CULTURE : ORGANISATION PARADIGM

Library management has to create its organisational structures and process that will encourage greater collaborative environment. Collaborative culture does not mean only cooperation and communication among the individuals working in the library. It signifies a collaborative environment which encourages, integrates and relies upon individuals for uniting ideas and implementing them into activities by exchanging views and learning from one another and in this way creating a product that otherwise could not possible. In such collaborative environment individuals are motivated to establish a community within which ideas are generated and implemented through operational activities not for personal gain or credit but for the organisation as a whole and its goals.

Schrage observes that "the act of collaboration is an act of shared creation and/or shared discovery... if one truly believes that organizations succeed by profitably amplifying the talents of their workers, then the challenge is to create collaborative tools and environments...[These] will become the sinews of organizational strength and personal development." Thus, collaborative culture is something more than just cooperation and collaboration, it is the creation of organisational culture as a guiding force to achieve the goals.

Collaborative culture can be created and maintained within the organisation by available information technology and personal expertise leading to build collaborative community. Such community can take the responsibility of major restructuring of library organisation around a new paradigm. The management of the library depending on a large number of manual files, hierarchical order, scaler chain, organisational chart, vertical administrative control and segmented administrative compartmentalisation having characteristics of an assembly line approach as in traditional library structure cannot be operative and functional in an electronic library environment. Collaborative community can work properly in a free, flexible interdependent and open minded environment.

Barbara I. Dewey and Sheila D. Creth opine that "The ultimate objective should be to shift to an organization philosophy and processes that will create intersections throughout the organisation to accomplish work, to communicate information, to train and develop staff, to resolve problems, and to encourage collaboration in order to deliver the most effective and dynamic service possible in a timely manner." In such information environment the concept of networked organisation with multiple relationships spanning the divisions to each of the units has to be implemented. It is also essential to create working relationships with work groups based on horizontal connections. Such operational network among different workgroups can utilise the staff resources efficiently and this will encourage creativity, enthusiasm and operational success having multilayered interaction and collaboration.

Individuals can innovate but innovation flourishes

in team oriented environments. Kanter states that "Organisations that are change-oriented, then, will have a large number of integrative mechanisms encouraging fluidity of boundaries, the free flow of ideas, and the empowerment of people to act on new information." According to Peter Drucker the strengths of the team-based organisation design are that it is receptive to new ideas and new ways of doing things, that there is great adaptability, and that it is the "best means available for overcoming functional insulation and parochialism." He opines that the team should task-oriented and advises "train them; recruit on the basis of teamwork potential; pay them for performance; and clean up the bureaucracy around them."

The team-based structure in the library may consist of both permanent teams and temporary teams as well as the individuals who have the creativity and expertise in specific areas or projects. For the operational system of the library individuals should not matter, it is important who are essential to constitute the team for delivering results and, in that sense, individuals may come and individuals may go. The team design should be based on bringing together the persons with a range or knowledge and skills to be applied towards specific activities and assignments. Leadership is required within a team but not to give commands. He has to decide who has particular responsibility to perform the task and authority is task-derived and task-focused, but the entire team will be responsible for the results.

In her article "Implementing Team Management in the Modern Library" (1990) Katherine W. Hawkins identified the following elements for successful team management.

1. Team members share responsibility for the effective functioning of the group.
2. Power and decision-making authority is shared by team members, with the team manager relinquishing control to subordinates when appropriate.
3. There is a balance of focus on both task and social maintenance behaviours.
4. Task responsibilities may be redefined in response to changing task demands.
5. Freedom from restrictive programmed decision-making encourages creative forms of decision- making.
6. Communication is lateral and vertical, spans the boundaries of the organization, and consists mainly of information and advice (from the vertical channel), and of consultation (from the lateral channels).

The team management should be responsible for planning, designing and decision making for the organisational and operational aspects of its own unit. The top management of the library will coordinate and oversee the planning and task operations of all the team management. In this way the whole management will not be certralised, library management as in case of the traditional libraries with strong line of command having organisational chart. This changed concept is that the unit with their own team management will be assigned specific tasks. Each unit will perform their own tasks and it will be fully responsible for delivering the results. All the tasks of all the units will be correlated and coordinated. Thus, the library, as a whole, will perform the functions. The management flow will be neither upward nor downward but the guiding force will be the final operational results through cooperation, collaboration and integration on the basis of individual motivation, skill, expertise and the spirit of attaining the final results.

In such situation the spirit of management comes from within the individuals and collaborative and shared responsiveness of the team. Therefore, management decisions do not come in vertical way, these come is lateral way. All the teams should follow self-management. In establishing self-managing teams extensive training must be provided to all staff members and specialised training must be arranged for groups with specilised assignments. Adequate education and training must be provided to team leaders to prepare them for the new environment.

Gerald R. Lowell and Maureen Sullivan describe their experience of Yale University Library in "Self-Management in Technical Services : The Yale Experience" (1990). They observe that "The benefits associated with self-management have already begun to be realized. Staff at all levels are actively engaged in problem-solving and are contributing in new and different ways. Some teams are already aggressively pursuing change to workflow in order to operate more effectively. Morale appears to be at a high level; the general atmosphere within technical services is positive and upbeat. Perhaps most astounding is that productivity has already increased." Team-based units having the responsibilities and authority perform the result-oriented tasks through self-management.

After the changeover to electronic environment the concepts of traditional library management, whether classical or scientific and even participative, have lost their relevance. In the computerised library situation files, records, notices and such other administrative records, all financial and accounting records, processing and technical services records, holding records, circulation records, information resources, and all other records are available to everybody on his computer screen.

Since all the information are available to everybody just on his table and everybody can contact anybody instantaneously, elaborate processes of carrying files and any hardcopy matter have been eliminated. Every record and document are available electronically. Therefore, decisions can be taken instantaneously.

Several universities is USA made experiments with the concept of team management in early 1990's. The University of Iowa Libraries first used team management in the collection development and management division, where thirty librarians started the jobs of assessing collections and acted as liaisons with the faculty members in specific subject areas. The primary focus was to provide a structure in which the librarians would determine how to share resources locally, avoid duplication of purchases, develop budget requests for the large number of subjects in each discipline, review decisions on electronic resources, and consult on various aspects of collection development and management. The next team was for the cataloguing department. A number of librarians with the assignment of the cataloguing department was involved in collection management activities, a link was established between both the teams.

The objectives of this reorganisation of library structure and management system for coordinated services were to redesign the administrative structure of the library, avoidance of repetitive jobs within a department or within more than one department, saving manhour and cost, resource sharing of various subject areas under a discipline and to streamline the task descriptions for efficiency and accomplishment of tasks in a time bound deadline. The immediate benefits were -

1. Removing the artificial and dysfunctional barriers between public and technical services and instead promote all activities as service for the users.

2. Providing a structure that should encourage, over time, greater collaboration among librarians in the delivery of services, and

3. Taking decisions at lower levels in individual units by encouraging lateral relationships and interactions rather than reliance on the hierarchy,

4. Creating a networked organisation which is in itself the most critical resource,

5. Motivating the library personnel to deliver appropriate results.

A different set of skills and attitudes is required among all the professionals including the supervisors. These qualities must be acquired before team organisation. Peters explains it in the way that "one of the most dramatic requirements associated with increasing responsiveness is to shift the organization's entire `way of being' from a `vertical' (hierarchical) to a `horizontal' (fast, cross-functional cooperation) orientation." In the managerial restructuring the role of middle cadre supervisors must be reconceived as one of "facilitator and functional-boundary smasher, instead of expert and guardian of functional units." The reason is that the middle cadre supervisors are expected to be the leaders of team management.

The team leaders must work with the purpose of incorporating a sense of responsibility among his co-workers for the overall results of the team effort by giving appropriate recognision and appreciation. Practically the team leaders need to create a personal influence rather than the authority vested in their positions. They have to cultivate a sense of commitment for cooperation and collaboration in all sphere of activities both by thinking and operating. The team setting requires all individuals to develop a high degree of self-discipline and responsibility towards all the activities and the fellow members and to make the joint effort successful. There must be clarity in communication and stability in decision-making. All members have to view themselves as having an essential contribution to make the group and to be united for a team approach to be successful. Individuals must feel welcome and connected to the group in the core.

It is a reality that a team model, while working, has to face many challenges at professional level and also personal level. All of them have to learn new skills and operational activities. They may have different expectations for responsibility and working relationships. But they should understand that in the team work there are potentialities for greater organisational innovation and personal development. The organisational structure draws on the team culture and values through collaboration. Within this environment mutual cooperation among co-workers can bring individual ideas and capabilities together to reach the common goal.

THE ELECTRONIC ENVIRONMENT

The goals of team work can be achieved only in the electronic environment. Computer-based communication and information technology offer the greatest opportunities for creating innovations in library and information services. Electronic communication systems can go far to increase efficiency and speed, capability and accomplishment of operational activities. Electronic communication can contribute to a distinctly different quality in interaction among library personnel. Thus, it can increase productivity of group-efforts.

Sproull and Kiesler, in their research "discovered a very high correlation between use of electronic mail and group productivity." They observe "Electronic group mail can decrease group coordination costs... The scheduling constraints of getting everyone into the same room at the same time vanish. Because electronic mail is asynchronous, everyone can "talk" at his or her convenience; everyone can "listen" at his or her convenience... Electronic mail... can approximate real-time interaction. Because electronic mail can archive the complete text of every message, the some group memory is available to every member." Electronic communication can go beyond the improvement of communication for existing groups and "more significantly, it can support groups and group activities that would be impossible and unimaginable without electronic group communication."

Electronic communication is the most important tool to allow the organisation to interact with the users for immediate and specific needs as well as to encourage collaboration that will lead to new products, services and directions for emerging needs. It also facilitate instant communication within the library as well as outside the library for administrative purposes and information exchange. The libraries must changeover from manual administration to electronic management to explore and exploit the human resources whether individual endeavors or group activities The electronic communication is a distinct departure from the limitations of traditional matter-based communication. The electronic interactive communication transforms the traditional communication ecology through remote access.

The availability of multipurpose high capability computer hardware, a variety of flexible software, networking and communication technology, enormous electronic storage capability and other innovative communication facilities have resulted unimaginable capability in electronic work environment. All the technologies are so interrelated, interdependent and potentially advancing that individual work cannot cope with their best utilisation, only group activities can exploit the best of their services in any organisation set up.

The technological innovations and electronic infrstructural facilities have changed our life, personal, economic, educational and societal, which we are compelled to accept. In such rapidly changing world we cannot afford to keep our libraries to be managed in the traditional way. The libraries and information centres must accept the new devices leading to electronic environment to make our services better and efficient and put ourselves on the new service track to become more up-to-date than our predecessors. We have to evaluate our work both in terms of quality and quantity and we should actively seek ways to improve on both. In the present situation we are sometimes called upon to change in response to circumstances outside the control of our organisations.

The technological changes in library management and operational areas should not be thrust upon the library situation by the top management or the library authority. It should come form within the library by the staff members as they are convinced and willing to accept the technological change. The library personnel at all levels should make good homework for the change and must be motivated and mentally prepared to changeover to electronic environment.

Usually the best ideas, technologies, efforts and processes fail if the people concerned are not psychologically involved and the people feel that they have no ownership of the problems or solutions, success or failure. Involvement and participation, responsibility and challenge are the most essential elements to employees feeling of ownership of the problems or solutions, success or failure. Involvement and participation, responsibility and challenge are the most essential elements to employees' feeling of ownership in planning, designing, experimenting, implementing and in achieving success. All these give the employees the sense of belonging, a sense of commitment to their activities. The electronic environment in the library needs all these elements along with the education, training, professional knowledge, skills and expertise. The human resource is the best resource in all the organisations.

At the very beginning of the planning stage participation and feedback must be taken from the library personnel and these are to continue throughout the change processes. In this way the management will gain credibility and trust. It can flow both ways by sharing information, thinking about changes, discussing ideas and exchanging cautions for anticipated failures.

Now, in our country, all the organisations, public or private, are finding that they must respond rapidly, both internally and externally, to new technologies and demands. Otherwise, they will lose their potential opportunities and will lag behind. The library personnel must understand the situation and should come forward for the change. When the authority will accept it the library personnel should have a real voice and sense of control over the affairs of change.

From manual to electronic environment, it is a total change by installation of hardware systems and peripherals, software selection, networking and other allied jobs, implementation of automated system and reorganisation of services. These are managed by committees, task forces, technical groups and other groups formed for the need to solve specific problems when they include representation from all units to be affected by a change. These are also mean for coordinating actions and processes across departmental lines. All the staff members should be involved in groups to design and implement a process to be implemented in respective units. The committees and groups should make deliberations in frequently held meetings formally. In addition to that personal interaction within units and cross-sections of groups are necessary to understand clearly a situation and to take decision. In planning, designing, organising and implementation team approach is required to solve problems and taking decisions as well as to operate whole system.

9

EFFECTIVE MEETINGS

Meetings do not fail, people fail who do not participate in the meetings effectively. Meetings are essential ingredients of all organisations for all times both at planning and decision-making stage as well as implementation and operational stage. The compelling reasons for library professionals are the operational issues, productivity issues, scope of change, enhancement of efficiency and to make the services result-oriented. The updatedness of information services and emerging trends of organisational structure and culture require crucial decision-making and its implementation. It can be done by collective wisdom, an effective result of successful meetings. For any decision information must be shared, all the aspects of an issue must be discussed, all the opinions must be considered, problems must be identified and solutions must be suggested and finally a decision must be arrived at. Meeting is the forum for such activities.

MEETINGS : THE NEGATIVE ATTITUDE

There are some inhibition regarding usefulness of meetings in the organisations; sometimes expressed and sometimes unexpressed. Mostly it comes from frustration among the staff members. There may be some valid reasons for frustration but their reasons for frustration lie with the conveners of the meetings, the chairpersons and the participants attending the meetings. Sometimes meetings are not convened in proper and appropriate time, chairpersons may not conduct the meetings in the right directions properly and the participants, sometimes wrongly selected or they do not participate or interact meaningfully. Negative attitude may be created for the following situations:

Lack of purpose or focus in meetings

Poor organisation of the meeting

Right persons are not invited or wrong persons are invited

Lack of specific decisions in the meetings

Actions not taken on the resolutions of the meetings

Feeling of disruption to other responsibilities

Lack of seriousness in attending meetings

Feeling of wastage of time if proper decisions are not taken

Conflict between supervisory staff and subordinate staff

Belief that meetings do not provide real opportunity to individual views

Dominating views suppress justified views

Inability to present ideas concisely

Lack of efficient leadership and control

Too many interruptions and digression

Mixed final decisions or inconclusive discussion

Existence of hidden agenda to divert discussion

Issues are not identified properly

There is truth that such situations occur, but meetings should be viewed as integral and essential ingredient to organisational life and culture. It is important to see that these constraints are avoided.

MEETINGS : THE POSITIVE RESPONSE

In the library situation, during the period of changing from manual method to electronic environment, known as changeover period, and during the electronic environment, known as operational period, meetings have a very crucial and vital role in organisation and management. At every step of planning, designing, organising, creating infrastructural facilities and decision-making meetings are most essential ingredients of library management. At the operational stage also meetings are concrete support to the library.

Meetings are a way of life in libraries and libraries have to accomplish the work with a number of persons with different perception. Their education, training, skill, professional expertise, way of thinking and personal traits are of a varied nature. Meetings become difficult and loaded with problems because the relationships among people, power and influence that exists within an organisation and difficulty of creating an environment in which individuals can speak openly about issues. However complex setting it may be, there is a considerable need to develop an understanding and skills to both plan and conduct as well as contribute to effective meetings. It is possible by focusing the meeting time in a constructive and creative way.

To make the meetings effective a different set of expectations and a different set of behaviours from everyone participating are required. These expectations and behaviours occur when the positive aspects of the meetings are in the mind with a strong determination to resolve the issues to be discussed. A commitment by both conveners of the meetings and participants is required to develop understanding and skill for using meetings successfully. There must be a willingness to exercise discipline and responsibility in every meeting.

Library meetings usually are held at different levels, among the persons at the top management for overall policy making, planning, creating organisational infrastructure, budgeting and financial resources, expenditure control, best utilisation of fund available, internal resource expenditure control, best utilisation of fund available, internal resource and external resource, human resource management, the shape of the library to come, improvement of existing services, design to be offered in future, and decision-making on other planning and implementations issues. Meetings are held between persons on top management and middle management or supervisors at various departments as well as between persons of middle management and subordinates at various levels. There may be meetings at departmental levels, section levels and unit levels as well as cross-sectional meetings and joint meetings at various levels.

Obviously, the objectives, purpose, agenda, issues and participant groups will vary from meeting to meeting, but these must be considered as the components of one organisation, the library. All the resolutions of all the meetings and their implementation, follow up activities and their results, further meetings, next follow up, next activities - all in a cyclic order will be leading to fulfil the objectives and to achieve the goals of the library. Convening meetings is a continuing process in the library for specific purpose, certain issues, necessary agenda, monitoring the resolutions and actions taken of the previous meetings. The resolutions and reports of the meeting are the embodyment of the blue prints and action plans of the library.

Considering the heterogeneous elements and attitudes of the library personnel it is to be admitted that in all spheres of library activities, as well as in the meetings, there will be differences of opinions, mode of work, identification of priorities, implementation of resolutions, and the best way to decide among many alternatives. Meetings get benefit from individual's knowledge regarding the issues and operations of the library as well as their knowledge of one another, this knowledge, on the other hand, may also a barrier in addressing problems or initiating new activities because of the differences in outlook, methods and priorities.

While there are meetings between supervisors and subordinates certain complex may work regarding the difference in power among those attending. Although everybody talks about working in a congenial environment with implied assumption of shared responsibility, it is no denying fact that supervisors retain considerable amount of power because of their position. It becomes harmful when they abuse or misuse such power. The supervisors must be aware of such danger and if they become reasonable, an environment can be achieved to exchange ideas, air disagreements, reach a decision and formulate agreement to perform the activities.

Another situation also arises when individuals come

to a staff meeting with their relationships already established from day-to-day contact. It is not expected that the participants of the meeting will alter their existing behaviour and attitude during the period of meeting on specific or sometimes controversial issues. They may reinforce their positions and suggestions may not be on real issues, but ego-centric.

But all these differences in opinions, attitudes, methods and point of view may be overcome by discussing the professional affairs and library interest outside the meetings, in day-to-day working situations and organisational environment. Meetings can be successful as a planning, problem-solving, decision-making and operationally capable vehicle if the operational environment is created in which personal respect and responsibility exist among all the staff members. Healthy disagreement about library affairs is honoured, divergent opinions and viewpoints are accepted as beneficial to the organisation. Successful meetings are the result of productive work environment.

Barbara I. Dewey and Sheila D. Creth suggest the following techniques to minimise factors that may have an adverse impact on staff meeting. These are :

1. Articulate outside of the meeting environment the expectations that staff are to work collaboratively with one another, to view themselves not as individuals defending their turf but as members of a team.
2. Establish a reward system that recognizes accomplishment of group efforts, not only individual efforts.
3. Begin each meeting with a statement that participants

will share responsibility for the quality of the meeting and that a variety of opinions are needed and disagreements are acceptable as long as they focus on issues, not personalities.

4. Rotate the responsibility for chairing or facilitating a regular staff meeting, since individuals are more likely to be supportive of colleagues knowing they will want this same support when they assume this role.

In the electronic environment a fundamental change occurs within library organisation. Manual library organisation is based on strict hierarchical administrative structure but electronic environment is essentially a network construction on the multidirectional network structure. In the network organisation, individuals work together to make planning, decision-making, system development, work flow, sharing responsibilities and problem solving regardless of sections, departments, division, position or status. In electronic environment network model emphasises the use of people's talent, skills, expertise and professional knowledge to tackle the problems and to come to solutions by innovative approach to service through collective efforts. Cooperation, collaboration and communication are essential ingredients in a network organisation leading to the commitment to the entire organisation. Job descriptions and activities are not limited to unit, section or department one belongs to, but to the library as a whole. Performance of jobs by individuals is not distinct and isolated contribution of the individuals, but a part of the united work force within the organised work structure. The feeling of shared responsibility creates the work pattern of the library on mutual understanding and respect.

MEETING TYPES

Meetings are held between management and staff, supervisor and subordinates, unit or section, in-charge and employees of that unit or section, among the colleagues, library staff and users or any kind of meeting convened with a particular purpose or issue. Whatever may be the kind of meeting, there must be specific necessity, purpose, content, agenda, priority of issues and concerned participants. Important factors are also the way the meeting is conducted, chair or leadership in the meeting, to what extent the meeting is beneficial to the library, the impact of the resolutions taken in the meeting. A meeting should be organised, convened, held and decisions made to support the management of the library, its operations and services. Every meeting must be successful. It is essential to recognise the objectives that meetings serve within the organisation. Any meeting may have a primary goal, but multiple goals also exist within the context of any one meeting.

Motivational meetings should be held for establishing and maintaining a sense of cohesiveness, cooperation, commitment and enthusiasm among a group of library staff working at any level. This type of meeting provides ample opportunities for ideas and views to be contributed by all members of a department or group of persons working together. Those who are directly involved with departmental activities can have dialogue frequently and this provides individuals with a sense of being a member of a team that is working together to achieve a particular goal. This sense of involvement ecourages them to be more skillful and professionally knowledgeable. At any organisational and operational stage there might be some problems to discuss or requirement of taking important decisions. The occasional meetings provide the opportunity to face any situation in a collaborative manner and share the feelings and wisdom in the interest of the library. There may be official agenda or not, such working relationships enhance staff morale. The continued interaction and commitment encourage group responsibilities.

In large libraries personal contacts with all the staff members is not possible. There may be psychological gaps between management and the staff members. A number of meetings can give opportunities to most of them to know the programmes undertaken or to be undertaken, the reasons for taking such programmes and the operational responsibilities of individuals and the groups. Everybody can hear the leadership directly, even if, instructions or memorandums have been issued. The staff members not only hear the persons in management, they can interact and give suggestions. By this way the staff members can feel that they are also part and parcel of the organisational set up, regardless to their positions in the library. Before planning the meeting a framework for structuring the meeting according to particular purpose in terms of agenda and participants must be made with a view to establish the desired result and its implementation.

Planning meetings consist of strategic long-term focus, medium-term planning and short-term needs. Planning meetings are held for policy making to be implemented in phases for overall organisation and management. Such meetings centre around new services, technical aspects of operations, new directions, new products and fixing priorities. Long-term planning or strategic planning suggests the broader organisational context with a timeframe of about five years. The planning models may be suggested considering all the aspects of the library and these models may be placed for consideration and to select one with or without modifications. Recommendations for the models may be obtained from persons at the top management, heads of the divisions or the departments, external experts, the library personnel with skills, expertise and technical knowledge and those who have hands-on experience. Series of meetings will be required to get the clear focus to issues concerned and to coordinate the planning process. Medium-term and short-term planning is usually made at departmental level having consultation with the top management and in accordance to the long-term planning.

Information or briefing meetings are held to provide adequate information to the persons concerned about the decisions taken at top management level and updated information about activities and programmes undertaken. These meetings are usually called by the management and supervisors to make the library staff aware regarding the idea of planning, decision taken, operational systems or probable constraints, if any. Such meetings do not proceed one way, the participants for whom the meetings have been convened should have the opportunities to clarify certain points and to ask questions about policies, implementation procedures, operational difficulties and any other matter. The conveners of such meetings and the senior position supervisors should explain all the issues raised and clarifications sought.

Problem identification and solution meetings are held in the libraries for a wide variety of issues. These may be workflow problems, communication problems, technical problems, complaint regarding service. When the problems are not solved at individual level and the problems relate to more than one individuals and work units, it is better to convence such meetings for identification of the problems, methods of solution and clarification of the ways by which solutions can be achieved.

The conveners of such meetings should first clarify the problems and the probable reasons for creation of such problems. Obviously, appropriate persons are to be invited. There must be sufficient time to discuss all the aspects of the problems. Depending on the problems and complexity of situation, the matter should be discussed till the solutions are explored. All the participants should be asked to consider all aspects of the situation to ensure that the real problems are addressed. Finally the solutions will be reached which will be accepted by all.

Conflict resolution meetings are required for disagreements between individuals. It may happen for differences of opinions, procedural questions, methods of activities, identification of priorities or any other reason. Disagreement may be between supervisor and subordinate, among members of the management, between library staff and user and between co-worker. In such situations focus should be given on the issue in particular and should go beyond the personalities of the individuals. Whatever may be the situation, conflicts must be resolved as early as possible, otherwise the library will be affected.

MEETINGS : PARTICIPATIVE COMMUNICATION

A broad understanding of communication techniques by library professionals is fundamental to successful meetings of all types and all formats. Effective interpersonal communication with understanding the effects of group dynamics in the meeting environment will help ensure successful meetings. The context of communication has four dimensions : Physical, social, psychological and temporal. The context is very important in behavioural attitude and patterns. An understanding of dynamics of interpersonal relationships can guide both conveners and participants know reacting behavior. Audrey Fisher and Donald G. Ellis define communication as "a pattern of behaviours in which the acts of each communicator constrain and are constrained by the patterns created by his or her own and others behaviors. All people who engage in communication develop an interdependent relationship with one another." Knowing the patterns of behaviours lead to develop successful strategies for achieving results. All kinds of behaviour are communication and any behaviour has a message value.

Communication implies a relationship between persons by both verbal and nonverbal methods of delivering message. Verbal Communication is discrete, consisting of words and sentences having a beginning and an end. Nonverbal Communication is not discrete but very powerful medium for transmitting all kinds of intended and unintended messages contained in facial expression, posture, movement of body or a part of it and showing an attitude. Nonveral communication may be continuous and does not have a discrete ending like verbal communication. Nonverbal Communication can be transmitted through one's body language, facial expressions, through using space for interpersonal communication, way of verbal communication such as, loudness, pitch, inflection of speech, speed or pause in between words, tone, way of putting the words and pronunciation of words. These elements of nonverbal communication may be used to make the intended opinion understand. The same sentence may be said in a positive manner or sarcastically depending on these elements. The participants of a meeting can understand each other's language, attitude or reactions very clearly through nonverbal communication.

In the meeting environment a group of persons communicate and exchange ideas, opinions, concepts, remarks and suggestions verbally and nonverbally. The discussion on any issue may be effective or ineffective. It depends on the interpersonal communication on that particular issue whether it will be resolved or not. Dewey and Creth have identified the following characteristics of effective interpersonal communication in the meeting environment.

Openness

A willingness to reveal information about one's views and opinions relevant to the topic and a willingness to react honestly to other's comments and ideas. Recognition that disagreement is not unusual within a group of people and that allowing differences to surface is productive as groups work toward conclusions.

Empathy

An understanding of what other individuals are feeling and their perspective on issues and concerns; an attempt to understand rather than more quickly to judge.

Supportiveness

Building a nonthreatening environment where others' comments are not attacked but critically analysed.

Positiveness

Holding a positive regard toward oneself and others, and creating a positive atmosphere that allows for productive encounters instead of negative and destructive ones.

Equality

Honoring every participant as a valuable and worth

while human being with something to contribute. Equality of respect is what is required no matter what the participant's status within the organization or the meeting setting.

These characteristics encourage participants to interact in a more positive manner and productive way. If the participants exhibit these characteristics collectively, the result will be more cohesiveness and mutual trust in the process of problem-solving and decision making. Such collaborative attitude will serve the interest of library in a meaningful way.

All the participants in a meeting including the convener cannot be equally aware about the issues discussed in the meeting. Everybody can highlight the problems and can suggest the methods or solutions in his own way but somebody has to take the leadership during the discussion with his knowledge, professional experience, expertise and capability to lead the discussion. Such person or persons must have the quality of personal interactions with credibility. The personal credibility of the leading participant in a particular meeting can be responsible for coming to solutions. The credibility of an individual can be achieved by his competence, character, intention, personality and dynamics. Competence is the knowledge and intelligence having professional or technical expertise. Character is the honesty and trustworthiness of a person. Intention is the attitude to work with sincerity of purpose. Personality is the quality of leadership with good understanding to make an impact over others because of general acceptability. Dynamics is the forcefulness and extrovertion to lead in spite of adverse situation. These qualities of a person or persons with objective approach can guide the other participants to reach a solution. Feedback in the meeting is an essential ingredient for anälysing the chain of events and decision-making.

MEETINGS: GROUP DYNAMICS

Meetings are the interpersonal communication of individuals assembled in groups for particular purpose to take decisions unanimously or by majority. The fundamental factor is interdependence which is the most important characteristic of group dynamics and roles. The group can function with individuals having a number of similar characteristics. Groups tend to take on a life of their own. The group identity is a powerful force regulating the behaviour of individual members to maintain and perpetuate the group identity. The group with any number of individuals accomplish the purpose of a meeting or a number of individuals accomplish the purpose of a meeting or a number of meetings, as required. But the most important factor is taking decision on particular issues for which a meeting is convened. Meetings may be held by a group for temporal issues or by a group for a particular period of time such as, committees, working groups, task forces, and the like.

In the meeting environment a group of individuals communicate with each other on individual issues. The deliberations in the meeting are affected by the degree the members show their interest, involvement, influence, expertise, knowledge and decision-making attributes on the issues under discussion. The interpersonal communication and interaction of the individuals on the issues are important factors. The individual members who have the most relevant information or creative ideas to contribute to decisions or to solve the problems can carry through in the meeting.

The role of individuals in a group is the prime factor as any group consists of a number of individuals. The individual's role can shift and completely alter the outcome and quality of the meetings. It happens on specific issues, methods of activities, identification of priorities, and such other factors. But two basic functions need to be balanced to take the decisions. These are (1) accomplishing the task, and (2) maintaining communication in order to ensure that the task will be accomplished. Sometimes, individuals act on a set of roles and attributes with them by virtue of their position, status and influence to act upon decision-making. In this way, various roles assumed by individuals affect the balancing act. But it should also be remembered that these elements may shift and change over time in groups or committees.

Dewey and Creth observe "Everyone plays a variety of roles each day. These role occur as a result of interaction in specific situations. Within the library organisation, librarians hold different roles, often simultaneously, such as :

* **Prescribed role :** usually denotes position, such as reference librarian, head of cataloguing, or director of the library. This role carries with it certain expectations not attributable to the position.
* **Earned role :** bestowed on a librarian as the informal leader or spokes person for a specific group or purpose. An articulate member of the reference department frequently called upon to provide the "reference" point of view is an example.
* **Functional role :** usually designated in advance and includes meeting convener, participant, and neutral facilitator."

The role or roles of individuals are determined by the purpose and the issues in the meetings. An individual can act in different roles in meetings convened for different purposes. Prescribed roles are significant in departmental meetings where the departmental head is, by virtue of his position, the leader of the meeting. Ascribed roles are important and crucial at the meetings of working groups, task force and other group meetings with specific purpose, such as library automation, selection of hardware an software, catalogue format and cataloguing, circulation, information storage and retrieval, and the like, where the value of expertise is most important. Earned roles are beneficial if respected professionals and retired persons with knowledge take part in informal meetings as experts. Such personalities with prominent roles can guide the meetings and help the group to achieve the goals.

Keeping in mind the group dynamics and individual roles in the meetings the participants of meetings should give proper value to cohesiveness which is the overall factor for decision-making. The attractiveness of a group to an individual will depend on the extent to which the group and participation in the group satisfies certain needs of the individuals. Cohesiveness develops a commitment to work together for a mission and a goal. The degree of cohesiveness affects the quality of the interaction within a group. Cohesiveness brings proper and appropriate communication in group dynamics and among individuals by which the individuals in a group can be committed to group goals and, thus, group goals can be accomplished even above personal roles.

In meeting environment there is a group, as a whole, and the participants as individual with individual traits. The balance of the role of individuals within a group meeting may be oscillating depending on the interpersonal relationships and strong individual opinions. When the opinion differs regarding process, methods, decisions in any situation, the meeting becomes time-consuming, confusing and directioness. In such situation the following suggestions may be helpful to guide the meeting on the right track.

* At the beginning the issues or problems should be identified, the group should have a focus and the meeting should be directed to the specific target. The appropriate context should be clear to all the members to provide a guideline for decision-making process.
* Diverse viewpoints, if any, should be invited so that tunnel vision can be avoided. Contrasting opinions should be honoured. In both the situations the individuals should be made understand with facts and arguments.
* The nature of the problems or the issues should be clearly stated and the purpose of the meeting should be explained.
* All alternative solutions should be considered and the best one should be determined.
* Each proposed solution should be evaluated properly discussing the positive and negative sides, so that the individuals can understand the reasons for not taking the solution.
* When a decision is to be taken as resolution it should be unanimously accepted.
* The convener and participants should not rush to a resolution prematurely without carefully articulating the problems and identifying the issues. This process

of meetings will increase cohesiveness and mutual respect.

The gaps in adequate communication and the complexities of personal interactions are the facts which occur. But these situations should be avoided as much as possible by cooperation. Meetings must be held in libraries as organisations. If the meetings are to contribute towards organisational effectiveness and personal satisfaction, considerable efforts should be made to understand group mechanics and the personal interactions. Certain values should be incorporated in the approach to organisational issues and working relationships among individuals. These are :

1. Willingness to place the needs of the library over personal or departmental preferences or needs.
2. Openness to different ideas, viewpoints, and personal styles.
3. Willingness to listen to and consider other's opinion and perspective.
4. An acceptance that disagreement over issues is healthy.
5. Generosity of spirit in working with co-workers.
6. Acceptance of responsibility for the quality of every meeting in which one is a participant.

These values should be the guiding force for improvements in the meeting process. The participants in the meeting environment whether in group or as individuals can utilise the meeting time effectively and can come to right decisions and, thus, the goals of the library will be achieved.

10

Performance Evaluation

Performance evaluation of the library personnel is an onging and continuing activity. This must be done for all the employees of the library at all levels on the basis of the individual's performance. Performance evaluation is not limited to a particular time-frame. It must be done as formal review which must be done as continuous monitoring in the light of objectives and goals of the library. Proper performance evaluation guides the accomplishment of goals by improving communication as well as understanding among the people working in the library. It also supports a positive work environment through improvement in the activities. As performance evaluation and review are ongoing activites for all the persons at respective levels, everyone will have a clear understanding of the responsibilities, objectives, goals and job standards. All the people will have the knowledge of how their tasks support overall activities of the library.

The term 'Performance Evaluation' is used interchangeably with 'Performance Appraisal' and 'Performance Review.' The terms signify the evaluation of tasks assigned to a particular person, assessment of the jobs done, personal capability to work with efficiency, cooperation with co-workers in a particular work environment and successful completion of work within a period of time set aside by the supervisor. The statement of evaluation is an official record regarding the performance of an employee. Performance evaluation is a day-to-day record compiled weekly and monthly and finally annually with comments of the supervisor. Performance evaluation report must be made available to the person concerned.

OBJECTIVES OF PERFORMANCE EVALUATION

Performance evaluation is a continuing process in management functions. Such evaluation reports contain vital information to improve and sustain library activities on the basis of both personal performance and group performance. Various activities of the library are directly influenced by the performance evaluation. It is the predictive information by which the activities, operations and strategies of the library can be redsigned.

Performance evaluations may reveal the quality of activities of both existing employees as well as newly appointed persons. If the evaluation reports indicate low quality of performance, necessary administrative steps may be taken. In case of newly appointed employees the selection process may be remodelled. Performance evaluation may reveal that the ongoing training programmes are not properly conducted and in some cases additional training is needed. It may be used as guidelines for future library planning. It may reveal that some departments are overstaffed and some are understaffed. Some persons may be more useful in some other departments with changed or new assignments.

Performance reviews can support in assessing future

personnel requirements and the concomitant skills required to support the library activities. Performance of activities depends on the right person with the right task in the right situation having right environment. If a person does not get the right task suitable to his qualification, expertise, motivation and job satisfaction, the person will be misfit to the jobs and ultimately the library activities will be affected. At the manpower planning stage the library tasks and the persons required should be matched. Performance evaluation of individuals can rectify such situation by modification or change of tasks.

Performance evaluations of all the employees of the library reveal the human resource employed and the library activities in totality. The library budget can be prepared considering the human resource and the library services. Creation of new posts, promotions, on-the job training and reallocation of jobs can be indicated in budget proposals. Performance evaluation and the manner in which such reviews are conducted have deep impact upon an employee's attitude towards the library and the specific tasks. Since performance review is conducted for all the individuals at all the levels, any employee and his supervisor are under review at all levels. The review process is an evaluative one and, at the same time, it indicates the development functions of the library. But it cannot be denied that there is a scope of inter-personal tension in the evaluation process. In human resource management it is a very delicate area because at every situation a person is an employee under a supervisor and, at the same time, that supervisor is considered as an employee under his respective supervisor. This situation prevails beginning from the lowest position to the highest position in upward direction in the hierarchical order.

The library managers at all levels must be aware of such situations and must sort out any state of tension or any problem. These areas can be eased through discussion, mutual cooperation, effective communication and understanding of respective situations. The purpose of performance evaluation may be stated as follows :

1. The individuals can understand the level of performance required to meet the job requirements and they know what types of performance are considered satisfactory or unsatisfactory.
2. They are informed about the quality of work currently being performed by them as well as the attitude of the mangement regarding their work. They can also understand whether the jobs done meet the standards that have been set.
3. The employees can identify the areas of activities that need improvement and such improvement leads to efficiency.
4. The evaluation reports become important communication channels between an employee and the supervisor. Many problems can be solved and constraints may be overcome by formal and informal discussion.
5. The management can identify outstanding performance and also can identify the areas of defficiency.
6. The good performers can be rewarded and this can be incentives to good performers. The performance reports may be considered at the time of promotion, job distribution and new assignments. It will strengthen the motivation of bad performers.

7. Performance evaluation only evaluates the task performance of individuals, it identifies deficiencies of the organisation as a whole. If the objectives and goals are not properly defined to the library personnel, planning cannot made to achieve the goals of the organisation, infrastructural facilities are not adequately offered, manpower planning is not well-thought, workflow is not properly designed, the capability of the individual employees cannot ensure running the organisation efficiently. Performance evaluation reveals the deficiencies of the management also. These may happen for the following reasons:

(a) Poor planning of library activities and operations,

(b) Bad and inefficient manpower planning for the library as a whole,

(c) Right persons are not appointed to the posts. Such situation may happen if screening of the candidates is defective, intentionally or unintentionally, favouritism is made in selecting candidates for appointments, knowledge, qualification, expertise, skills and personal capability for the vacant posts and promotional posts are improperly assessed,

(d) Poor supervision on the part of supervisors. They may not have interpersonal skills, may not be good task masters, may show discriminatory behaviour or may not distinguish between good performance and bad performance because of lack of leadership qualities,

(e) Inadequate orientation and training of the library personnel can cause inefficiency among the staff members,

(f) Poor working condition due to interpersonal conflicts,

non-working requirement, non-supply of necessary requisites, lack of administrative support and bad work environment can cause inefficiency on the part of individuals.

KEY ELEMENTS IN PERFORMANCE EVALUATION SYSTEM

Performance evaluation system must have certain prerequisities which are the key elements of the evaluation system. To make the system most effective and result-oriented, the tasks of the individuals under evaluation system and the standards used in evaluation must be clearly defined. Both the employee and the supervisor must understand the tasks and the evaluation standards. The key elements are stated below :

1. The library must have performance evaluation policies and procedures approved by both library committee and library authority to make the evaluation system consistent, uniform and fairly conducted. The policy statement must be printed and make available to all the employees. It must contain the position of the supervisor who will conduct the evaluation process and what are the criteria of the evaluation. The written procedures must be available to both the supervisors and the employees. Both of them should ensure that the evaluation process is conducted consistently, uniformly and competently. Such recorded evaluation policies and procedures can be used as guidelines for training evaluators.

2. The library must have written job descriptions. The term job description includes all aspects of the jobs of individuals to be performed, tasks to be performed, abilities, skill and knowledge needed for all the jobs expected from the employees. The job description

consists of the basic tasks to all the tasks entrusted to a person, to all the jobs assigned to an individual either to be performed individually or sharing one's role with other employees as required in the library. Job description depends on the job analysis. It is the process by which the tasks and activities of each job are identified. The end-product of this process is the job description. Job description of an individual is a coherent part of the unit of employees concerned. Job analysis is conducted without reference to a particular individual who may perform the job. It is the smallest unit of the total library activities and operations. It can be performed by any individual at any point of time. Job analysis is percieved as distinct from persons performing the jobs. The tasks are defined in job analysis and tasks are described in job description. Either an existing employee performs the job or someone has to be recruited for this purpose. The overall function of the job analysis is to identify objectively the tasks required to perform specific jobs. After the job analysis specific tasks are described in job description to be performed by an individual. In job description the details of the responsibilities of each position is enumerated. In the performance evaluation process, both the employee and the evaluator must have a clear idea regarding the rate of success or failure of performance of the jobs.

3. The library must have performance evaluation forms in standard format to assure consistency. These forms must be distributed among all the library staff without considering the designations. The forms should include all the required and relevant items for performance evaluation of the individuals with clear instructions as needed.

4. The library must have evaluation training programmes. The performance evaluation process is complex, difficult and on-going process. Various administrative factors, infrastructural situations, availability of tools and gadgets, environmental conditions, work situations, budgetary constraints, intra-human relationship, service conditions, and other factors play an important role in performance evaluation of an individual. Objective and quantitative evaluation based on the evaluation forms may not reflect the actual performance. The supervisors cum evaluators should have substantial training before conducting performance evaluation. Evaluation process should be both quantitative and qualitative. Printed training manual or instructions should be available for this purpose. Library staff should be oriented for evaluation process.

GUIDELINES FOR EVALUATION

Performance evaluation is the process of evaluating the relative capability or worthiness of an individual employee against pre-determined, job-related performance standards set by the job description or individual position. Such evaluation is formal and systematic. Employees are aware that they are being evaluated and being told the criteria that will be used in the process of evaluation. Performance evaluation includes generating useful information about the employees and the actual nature of the duties as described in job descriptions. Such data should be incorporated in the human resource planning document for the purpose of career planning, distribution and re-arrangement of job allocation and positions in future as well as for identification of needs for training and development. It helps the supervisors and subordinates at every stage to investigate problems jointly. It also creates an environment which helps subordinates in their motivation and involvement and creating an effective system within the library's management information infrastructure.

Performance evaluation will bring the following results:

1. It will define the specific job criteria against which performance will be evaluated.
2. It will enhance performance in current job.
3. It will accurately measure post-job performance.
4. It will indicate the development experience the employee needs in a particular work situation.
5. It will prepare the employees to qualify for future higher responsibilities.
6. It will provide an aggregate work standard as a profile of the library in terms of its human resource strengths and weaknesses revealing the employee's skills and experience.
7. It is indicative of total evaluation of the human resource of the library.
8. It is the vital instrument to be used by supervisors at any level to encourage, motivate, train and reinformce the jobs of their subordinates.

Performance evaluation is the core element of the human resource management in the library. Performance of the individual employees, time-bound work done in an unit, section or department of the library and meaningful service of the library are revealed in the performance evaluation reports. The progress of the library or the regress, if any, is reflected in these reports. The success or failure of the library, meaningful role in the parent organisation and efficient service pattern practically depend on the library personnel on the basis of individual as well as collective performance. Therefore, performance of individual employees is the most vital factor. Evaluation process is an important tool to analyse the human resource for the following reasons:

(a) it provides adequate feedback to each individual regarding his performance,

(b) it serves as a basis for improving or changing behaviour pattern towards more efficient and effective job performance,

(c) it provides data for required changes in job assignments.

At each level of hierarchical order of the library personnel there are supervisor and employees under him. The supervisors should advise the performance related to objectives of the library, performance improvement by individuals by advising what is expected of the employees, counselling for effective job performance and intra-personal relationships for better cooperation. To achieve these ends the following steps should be taken.

1. Estabilishment of performance standards,
2. Communication to employees regarding performance expectations,
3. Measuring of actual performance,
4. Comparison between actual performance of individuals with the standard set for this purpose,
5. Discussion with the employees regarding evaluation results,

6. Taking corrective steps as and when necessary,
7. Performance evaluation should be an open and honest affair between the supervisor and the employees.

In the process of performance evaluation the vital and crucial consideration is the ethics of evaluation and its openness. Otherwise, there might be many organisational problems, deterioration of intra-personal relationships, ego-clash, fall of efficiency and such other situations. All the library personnel must know the reasons for performance evaluation, process of evaluation, result of evaluation and they must be convinced that the evaluation is essential both for the persons as well as for the institution. Performance evaluation should be both qualitative and quantitative.

PERFORMANCE EVALUATION PROGRAMME

Performance evaluation programme is on-going activity for each supervisor at all levels leading to organisational success. The programme is not limited to annual, formal review of the job description of an individual, it is continuous monitoring of all the library personnel to achieve the organisational goal and to fulfil the library objectives. Performance evaluation is not just the review of work of individuals. It aims the accomplishment of achieving the goals through understanding the work environment and by improving communication among the library personnel leading to positive work situation. The supervisors at each level of the hierarchical administrative order are responsible for performance evaluation of the subordinates. Therefore, library personnel at all the levels must have clear understanding of their job descriptions, responsibilities and performance standard. All of them must know how their tasks support the departmental activities leading to fulfillment of the objectives of the library.

To make the performance evaluation programme most effective and result-oriented, the tasks under review at all levels and the standards set determined for the purpose must be clearly understood by the supervisors and subordinates at all the levels. The responsibilities of each employee is communicated by formal performance evaluation forms available for this purpose which records position description as well as job description. The functions, tasks and responsibilities of an employee are given in detail in the form to understand the tasks and the standard of performance expected. The supervisor should explain the position description and questions concerning the tasks and duties should be discussed. The position description and the responsibilities must be clearly understood by the concerned employee. The supervisor should remain objective and unbiased to evaluate the performance of an individual.

Each employee should have clear understanding regarding the level of proficiency required for the various tasks enumerated in the position description. Attempt should be made to develop performance standard of each task. The individual employees should be consulted for this purpose. Sometimes, employees themselves can develop the performance standard from their own experience and experiments. All the tasks of an individual and employees of an unit should be discussed for exchange of ideas and experience. Supervisors of related units and the staff also should be consulted to find a better way and to ensure efficiency.

Supervisors at every level are responsible primarily for performance evaluation of his subordinates. The final evaluation is done by the library management. Supervisors must have close look over the performance of tasks and discharging the responsibilities assigned to them. The performance of tasks should be compared with the pre-determined standard. Performance of all the employees under him should be monitored closely and regularly. Supervisors should be objective in performance evaluation. They should not be victims of personal liking and disliking or external and internal pressure. Evaluation should be based on the tasks and responsibilities assigned to the employees. Completion of the tasks and discharging responsibilities within stipulated time-frame having effective result should be considered.

Supervisors must monitor the changes which may occur for many reasons. There may be changes in objectives and goals of the parent organisation, changes in library management procedure, changes in work environment, changes in staff pattern or changes in service pattern. Whatever might be the change, supervisors should evaluate the changed situation and they should determine to what extent the performance standards might be affected by such changes. While major changes such as, department reorganisation, establishment of new department, introduction of new services or total change because of library automation occur, management, supervisors and concerned employees should review the situation and recast the tasks, duties and responsibilities of the concerned employees as essential in the changed work situations. But the position description and task responsibilities must remain clear and properly understood by everyone involved.

All the tasks should be completed within the time-frame scheduled. Supervisor must monitor daily tasks and progress of the jobs. He should advise employees throughout the year regarding completion of work schedules and quality of performance of the subordinates. If there is any kind of lacuna in job performance or lack of timeliness, the supervisor should draw the attention of the person concerned for rectification. Moreover, he should motivate and inspire the employees and create a sense of belonging to the library.

The role of all the library staff is also vital in performance evaluation. All of them must take active role and participation in the performance evaluation programme. All the staff members should be involved in updating position descriptions, updating performance standards and in setting performance objectives. Supervisors should motivate the employees and should take corrective measures, if needed. Supervisors and employees at all levels should discuss all the aspects of performance evaluation, keeping in mind that the evaluation process is not only for the individuals, it is the performance evaluation of the library service as a whole to fulfil the objectives of the library.

The objectives of formal performance evaluation are:

1. to provide a record of each individual employee regarding performance of tasks, duties and responsibilities assigned to him and his capability and motivation to perform according to pre-determined standard of efficiency as well as to assess to what extent he has been able to reach the standard set for the purpose, whether below, actual or above the standard.

2. to provide a record, in each case, on the basis of both qualitative and quantitative measurement. The record must be unbiased, objective, performance-oriented, impersonal and fact-based,

3. to allow consistency in documenting performance keeping evaluation standard identical to each person working at the same level,

4. to understand and determine the strength, weakness or constraints to reach performance standard in each case and to find the problem, if any, personal, work situation, lack of team spirit, dictation of supervisor, lack of understanding of a particular situation, and other reasons. Advice, suggestions and rectification methods should be recorded.

5. to provide methods and planning objectives and goals for the future.

The formal performance evaluation should be approached as a means of evaluating employee performance and developing strategies for improving personal performance as well as the performance of the library as a whole.

The performance evaluation programme consists of two methods, first, each employee must fill up Personal Evaluation Form, a format given by the library. The filled-in forms will be scrutinised by the supervisor. Secondly, each employee must appear before an interview board consisting of supervisor and other persons as entrusted by the library management. Before the interview board the employee can present his case regarding the statement he has given in the Personal Evaluation Form and his impressions about work situation. Performance evaluation will be based on the statement given in the evaluation form and the result of the interview.

For the effective and meaningful interview the following steps should be taken :

* Study the position description, know what the employee should be doing.

* Evaluate your performance as a supervisor, how you advised him in course of the work.

* Know past performance, critical incidents, and observations. Consider performance of the employee for the whole year.

* Know the contributions the employee has made and his potentialities. Did he work upto his maximum capability?

* Know the work environment of the employee and his reactions with co-workers.

* Allow him to tell frankly his impressions about the work situations, his motivation, his constraints, his difficulties.

* Listen carefully to the employee's comments, his assessment of job description and performance, whether he is satisfied with his own performance and his suggestions.

* Discuss areas for improvement both in the area of his own work and areas of co-workers. Does he require any kind of support from his supervisors? Include employee's comments in the evaluation form.

* Summarise major points, areas of improvement agreed, follow-up plans, support needed.

* Know the training or development programme needed for the employee. Set time-frames for measuring performance improvement. Follow the formal review with regular informal review to monitor progress on improvement.

The interview must be close-door, confidential and one person at a time. Formal evaluation forms must be kept under security and kept with individual personal files.

Performance evaluation is essential for human resource management. Supervisors can improve their ability to evaluate employee performance by remembering four points: listening, observing, understanding and discussing. Individual employees may have suggestions for improvement not thought by others. By monitoring performance, being aware of the work of each employee, resolving problems as they arise, and rewarding good performance as it occurs, the supervisor should ensure that both supervisor and employee have clear understanding of each other's responsibilities for fulfilling the objectives and for achieving the goals of the library and the parent organisation.

A programme without a systematic plan for evaluation cannot, over the long run, be realistically considered valid, promotable, or supportable from the management perspective. Without data analysis, identifying programme weaknesses and making improvement programme, no library can achieve the goals. All levels of management have an inherent responsibility to encourage, promote, and require programme and service evaluations, emphasising their positive, constructive value in improving the organisation and those in it. Good programmes and good performance must be recognised and rewarded. But it is more important that problems identified through performance evaluation must be solved positively and constructively.

Performance evaluation is a basic management practice consisting of a three-phase process. Each phase requires conscious consideration of several questions, factors and principles. The three phases are development phase, implementation phase and administrative follow-up phase.

In the development phase a systematic evaluation plan and strategy should be developed. Programme objectives and goals must be clearly articulated and understood. Careful attention should be given to the kinds of data that need to be collected in the evaluation process to answer questions about attainment of each and every stated goal.

In the implementation phase evaluation techniques are administered and data are collected. Implementation should be made by both formal evaluation with written instructions and informal verbal interaction.

The administrative follow-up phase is a continuing process of monitoring at every step to follow up the implementation process. Continuing administrative check up, formal and informal monitoring, understanding the problems of implementation phase and synchronizing all efforts to fulfil the objectives of the library by solving the problems and overcoming the constraints administrative follow-up phase works. The three phases work simultaneously.

11

MANAGEMENT LEADERSHIP

All successful organisations, even with dedicated and capable professional personnel, have got the success with effective leadership. An exceptional leader with vision and capability energises his organisation to attain its full potential and makes a real difference in the community. Extraordinary leadership is the key. The real leader inspires others with his right focus, real passion and, above all, the far-reaching vision. The right person has the sincerity of purpose, never-ending hope, bright inspiration, command of personality, control of resources, and, with all these he can move the organisation in the right direction. Leadership is a quality by which an individual or leadership team induces a group of persons to pursue objectives held by the leader. The leader can perceive what is needed and what is right and can mobilise people and resources to accomplish the goals.

At the top level, while it is management leadership, it is not just managing the organisation. The basic responsibility of a manager is to operate and maintain the organisation efficiently by ensuring that it provides useful services to the immediate public by utilising all the resources properly. The management leader does the same thing and, in addition to that, he is more concerned with building the organisation for the future, securing new resources, developing new capabilities, accepting new ideas, and using new technologies for adapting to change. The attention of the leader tend to be broader, both for the present and for the future direction to face any challenge for the potential growth of the organisation.

Managers tend to be problem-solvers by seeking better ways to deploy their resources to discharge their responsibilities. They are analytical thinkers using their judgements on performance evaluations, guide the workforce to do their best to achieve the goals of the organisation. Management leaders are more intuitive and divergent in their thinking to become the pathfinders as opposed to problem-solvers. They search for new directions beyond the boundaries of their own organisations. Burt Nanus and Stephen M. Dobbs observe "finally, the successes of managers and leaders can be evaluated on different scales. Managers are deemed successful when they operate the organisation efficiently, delivering services on time and within budget. Leaders are deemed successful when they enable their organizations to grow in their ability to serve the community, whether that be by discovering new community needs to satisfy, by expanding the resource base, by entrepreneuring new approaches to service delivery, or by energizing or transforming the organization itself". In an often-quoted phrase, "managers do things right, while leaders do the right thing". The libraries need both good leadership and good management to achieve the goals. Either one is necessary but not sufficient.

At any time, the management leader should have the focus in the following directions:

1. Interaction with the library personnel at all levels, users of the library, outsiders and vendors, members of the library committee and the library authority, experts, specialists, faculty members, and others, inside the organisation.

2. Inter-institutional relationships, access to local, national and global databases and information resources, communicating vendors at international level, establishing relationships with scholars and specialists outside the organisation.

3. Quality of service provided to clientele inside the organisation and outside the organisation on request, managing organisational structure, efficient workflow, all kinds of library and information services and deploying human resource in the most effective way.

4. Anticipating trends and development of innovations in new technologies and planning for their use in future services, important implications of the new information and communication technologies, developing the workforce and human resource to that direction, changes in aims and objectives of the parent organisation and their impact upon the future service pattern and to foresee the long-term strategy.

The management leaders have many roles to perform in their organisations. The abovementioned roles 1 and 2 are the roles of management strategist. Basically as management expert the leader is the person responsible to guide the organisation to the right direction, and for this reason he has to create and activate all infrastructural facilities required for the moving on. When all the physical resources are at hand, his crucial concern is the human resource. The right person must be at the right place for right jobs, who can deliver the result. While the physical resources and human resources match properly and meaningfully, the leader can move the organisation in the right direction. As management strategist the role of the management leader as direction-setter is crucial. To fulfil the aims and objectives of the organisation the management leader foresee the realm of future possibilities in the outside world seeking more desirable destination for the organisation.

Roles 3 and 4 are the roles of the visionary. With self-confidence and conviction the management leader infuses the vision to his people by clearly stating his vision so that others will be inspired to follow. The leaders have the visions, and when they are widely shared, the situation leads to organisational growth and progress. The efficient management leader is a super networker, a builder of interwoven relationships whose purpose is ultimately to provide useful resources, information and back-up support to serve all the target groups in the organisation.

The crucial role of the management leader is to become an efficient and successful coach. Leaders are inherently teambuilders. They choose, create and mature group of persons who share a similar vision, passion and sense of responsibility to support the leader in fulfilling the objectives. They build trust which is the bond that holds an organisation together. They inspire the individuals, the followers and help them learn, grow and realise their full human potential to serve the organisation.

The vital role of the management leader is the role of change agent. The leader sets the position of the organisation for the future. He makes critical choices or influence the decisions of the others about which services are most needed and which target groups among the clients should get the most attention. This may involve introducing a new programme or creating useful alliances or interrelationships with meaningful partners. Sometimes it involves restructuring the sections of the organisation or reconfiguring some aspects of service delivery. It involves major entrepreneurship and innovation, by which the nature of the organisation undergoes a transformation.

QUALITIES OF MANAGEMENT LEADERSHIP

Qualities of management leaders are mostly inherent having personal attributes of leadership. They are assertive, systematic and courageous. They are articulate and well-groomed. There have been many researches on the qualities which contribute most to leadership effectiveness over a period of several decades. G. Yukl in "Leadership in Organizations" (1994) states that the personality traits of leaders are high energy level, self-confidence and self-control, emotional maturity, integrity and ability to tolerate stress.

John W. Gardner in his "On leadership" (1990) reviewed the literature and observes that the desired qualities are the physical vitality and stamina, willingness to accept responsibilities, task competence, intelligence and judgement in action, understanding the superiors and subordinates of their expectations, determination to achieve the goal, skill in dealing with the people, capacity to motivate, steadiness in thinking and actions, capability to win and hold trust, confidence, dominating personality, assertiveness, adaptibility in any situation and flexibility of approach.

During 1980s and 1990s a large number of survey were conducted on thousands of junior and senior executives. The American management Association sponsored a number of studies to identify leadership characteristics. All these studies identified 225 leadership characteristics essential for successful leadership. Among them four characteristics were in the top of the lists in almost all the studies. These are competence, inspiring, forward looking and honesty.

Library, as a service organisation, requires leaders to be effective who can get things done. Whatever may be the administrative situations, or with inadequate physical resources, financial constraints, not that efficient library personnel- in all such situations the leader is expected to serve the users as effective as possible. Efficient leaders know their own strengths and weaknesses, and they are perpetual learners. The leaders should show self-confidence and take the initiative to control the events even in adverse situations, and should not merely react them.

We expect all the libraries should perform the activities in the same way. Unfortunately our experience is otherwise. The management leader in the library, who displays a passion for the effectiveness and possibilities of the organisation, can inspire others with his enthusiasm and sense of optimism and sets a good example, can be the inspiring leader. The quality of leader, as pointed out by R. W. Emerson "Not he is great who can alter matter, but he who can alter my state of mind". Subordinates respond well to the leader who appeals to their good nature and emotion, and inspire them for the service to the organisation.

Management leaders must have the vision for the near future as well as far future for which long-term planning is envisaged. The vision should not be a fixed one, it should be flexible according to the objectives of the organisation and goals to achieve in the ever-changing world. The target groups, their needs and requirements, their expectations, the ramifications of knowledge areas, the approach to library services, impact of new technologies upon all areas of library activities - all these factors must be in the foresight of the leader. All these help the organisation to grow and develop, therefore, all organisations seek leaders who are forward looking, visionary and persons of imagination with the capability of transforming it into reality. They can show the followers the way to brighter tomorrow. George Barnard Shaw said that we become wise not by remembering the past but taking responsibility for the future.

The leaders must earn the trust and confidence of the followers and they must be believed by them. They must be trustworthy with the faith regarding the integrity of the leader. He must be honest in words, behavior and activities. In this way the leader can expect the same qualities from the followers. The honesty of leader can motivate the subordinates to be honest and sincere in their habit and activities. The hint of unethical behaviour severely damages the human relationship and, as a result, damages the organisation.

With these major attributes the studies show that other qualities are determination, persistence, drive, courage, creativity, flexibility, decisiveness, and above all, charisma of personality. With the inherent qualities the leaders develop themselves and they are self-taught. They actively seek leadership responsibility, perform their job successfully and earn the right of leadership. In addition to learning from reading and experiences, the leaders learn by self-reflection. They can assess their own strengths and weaknesses to determine what to do and what not to do. They also learn from superiors in the family, teachers of academic institutions, seniors in service life and role models in the professional life. They also learn through personal experimentation by putting themselves in challenging situations. They learn through their whole life and prove themselves on the job. They demonstrate that they deserve to be leaders through leading their teams and by achieving the results.

Management leaders should be good askers as well as great listeners. If newly appointed, they can learn about the organisation by asking questions to the library personnel. The areas may be:

Mission of the organisation and its commitments

Suggestions regarding modification and redirection

Present work environment and service pattern

Weak areas in activities

Performance evaluation and its results

Rating of the activities and services

J. Lipman-Bluman (1996) conducted a ten-year study over five thousand leaders of various types of organisations. He identified nine basic leadership styles as a result of the study. Some leaders may follow several styles but everybody has his own distinctive pattern of leadership. The basic leadership styles are as follows:

"1. *Intrinsic*: The leader concentrates on his or her vision or task and measures progress strictly on those terms.
2. *Competitive*: The leader is driven by a passion to outdo competitors.
3. *Power*: The leader is driven by a need to control events and people.
4. *Collaborative*: The leader favors teamwork and collegiality.
5. *Contributory*: The leader is driven by a need to help others achieve their goals.

6. *Vicarious*: The leader encourages or mentors others.
7. *Personal*: The leader uses charm, wit, prestige, and other personal attributes to attract followers and persuade them to act.
8. *Social*: The leader networks extensively to form alliances (not what you know, but whom).
9. *Entrusting*: The leader selects capable people and entrusts them with his or her goals and visions."

All leadership qualities and leadership styles can be successful while the leaders have the vision proper to make advancement with confidence in the direction of their dreams. The old proverb is "If you don't know where you're going, you might end up some place else". A vision is a realistic, credible, attractive, and inspiring future for the organisation.

ROLES OF THE MANAGEMENT LEADERS

An organisation must have the mission, the vision and the strategy planning. Mission is the statement of why an organisation exists, vision is a statement of where it is headed, and strategy planning is a statement of how it intends to get there. Strategy is the overall frame work governing the decisions and actions to be taken by an organisation to realise its mission and vision. The strategy planning and decisions include introducing new services, expanding the service area, making existing services more efficient, offering new facilities, expanding user groups, creating cooperation and resource sharing, and making interrelationships with other organisations and institutions. These decisions need to fit into an overall pattern or framework to ensure that the resulting actions are consistent with each other and supportive of the mission and vision of the organisation. All leaders need strategies.

Strategies embody the shared goals and expectation of the organisation. Strategies make the basis for explicit actions, open to feedback and subject to improvement over time. They also create the foundation of relationships, both internal and external, because the leaders know that people should understand where they are leaded and they are getting there. The strategy planning must be designed to advance the mission of the organisation, but the best strategy planning also flow directly from a well-formulated vision statement. When strategic planning is designed to support a clear, shared vision of the future, it tends to be far more powerful as guide to action. Strategies are more innovative when they are driven by a vision of the future and decision makers are released from the constraints of habitual way of thinking and current practices.

Strategic planning allows strategic opportunities to be prioritised because they can be evaluated in terms of how they contribute to the attainment of the vision. Strategic planning and its transformation into activities are more likely to be mutually supportive when they all contribute to moving the organisation in a common direction. The strategies, thus, are most effective when they serve as the bridge between vision and action. The whole process of activities coordinate the authority, the leadership, the personnel, the target groups of users to a common set of objectives and goals. This coordination makes effective use of resources, concentrating them in programmes for effective and meaningful services.

Strategic planning is the way the organisation identifies and evaluates the strategic options flowing from its mission and vision; decides upon goals, objectives and plan of action; and implements them. Every organisation has its own approach to a strategy process, tailored to its own character and aspirations. The three initial steps of strategy process are:

1. Developing a mission,
2. Deciding on a strategic thrust,
3. Identifying the strategic issues to be resolved.

For developing the strategy process the following points are to be considered. A task force should be constituted to bring various perspectives in search for strategy process. The specially constituted task force can discover bold new approaches beyond the traditional way of thinking.

1. Appropriate time horizon is to be selected,
2. Needs to be included in the strategy process are to be specified,
3. The needs and requirements of various target groups, and potential needs in future and in changed situations are to be assessed,
4. Long-term trends affecting the strategy process are to be evaluated,
5. Strategic factors, problems, and opportunities are to be identified,
6. Strategic alternatives are to be created and evaluated,
7. The implementation plan must be devised. No strategy recommendation is complete without a clear statement of goals and objectives, and specific ways to measure the effects and results if the strategy is implemented.

The leader must be a strategist. The fact finding and planning tasks in reaching a strategy may be delegated to appropriate persons but the leader must ensure that an appropriate strategy for the organisation is formulated and implemented. The leader is to decide when a new strategy is needed. Whatever may be the stimulus for a new strategy, the leader is the key person who must initiate and champion the strategy process. He creates the necessary mandate and a common strategy process. He decides who will be involved in the process; and form the necessary work force for implementation of the strategy. The leader creates a sense of expectation about the results and a sense of priority and urgency during the whole process.

The leaders provide a great service for the strategy process when they spearhead the development of a mission, vision and strategic thrust to guide it. These steps are essential to inform and focus the strategy process and to set high standard, and to ensure that the resulting strategies will have some degree of coherence and consistency. Once the strategy process has begun in an organisation, the leader usually will be deeply involved to move it along and keep it on track. The leader's sense of optimism, confidence and wisdom in the implementation of the process can inspire and motivate others with the determination to carry the process to completion.

While the strategy process has been completed, the leader should ensure that the resulting strategy is fully implemented. Then all the pieces of the strategy are to be collected into a coherent whole to be presented to the authority. The leader is responsible for getting everyone's agreement, ensuring that everyone fully understands and supports the strategy. Then the strategy has to be communicated to all the persons concerned so that they can coordinate their actions with it. Throughout the planning process and implementation process, as long as the strategy is in effect, the leader serves as a role model, negotiator, spokersperson and coordinator. The leader must be ever vigilant to ensure that the strategy drives decision making and action throughout the organisation. As the implementation process proceeds, he monitors progress, analyses the constraints, and finally achieves accomplishment. Strategy is the instrument with which the leader determines how to renew or transform the organisation. In the words of Coleridge, the great English poet, who said that, "often do the spirits of great events stride on before the events, and in today already walks tomorrow," The successful management leaders can only feel the "spirits of great events".

The management leader in an organisation is the chief change maker. Warren Bennis in his work, "On Becoming a leader" (1989) defines the attribute of leadership as, "a leader is, by definition, an innovator. He does things other people haven't done or can't do. he does things in advance of other people. He makes new things. He makes old things new. Having learnt from the past, he lives in the present, with one eye on the future. And each leader puts it together in a different way". The condition of an organisation is the result of an unending struggle between continuity and change at any given time. Continuity characterises the steady, ongoing services provided by an organisation to its clientele of various target groups. The leader has to set high standards for service and see that the right people are put in charge of the affairs concerned, and that they have the necessary resources to perform the activities. He has to guide the persons and monitor the activities of all the persons concerned and to coordinate all the activities and operations.

Any kind of change presents a totally different set of circumstances, whether partial or total. Change characterises an organisation in transition. Any change, whether in the present activities or total change in the future, must be initiated by the leader and he is responsible for promoting it and ensuring that it happens in a way that is beneficial for the organisation. James MacGregor Burns observes in his work, "Leadership" (1978) that "the ultimate test of practical leadership is the realization if intended, real change that meets people's enduring needs". But it cannot be achieved easily.

Change, in any organisation, originates in the mind of the leader and then, it percolates in the minds of the people concerned. Every individual has his reactions to change which is not always welcome. The attitude to change is a mental state depending on the psychology of individuals. Sometimes it is welcome and accepted by some people and some people may react in a different way. Whenever there comes a proposal for change in the existing activities, operational procedures or organisation set up, some persons become apprehensive. They are accustomed to perform activities in a particular manner, habitual to particular work situation, and their mental state is set in that way. The proposal for change may create confusion, uncertainty and fear in their mind. Some people are genuinely threatened by change, especially if it disrupts activities they are habitual to do. They may feel uncomfortable because they are not sure which will follow the proposed change. They are not able to measure up the results which will accompany the change. Many people are afraid of change because they apprehend that the proposed change will complicate their jobs and their expertise and efficiency will not be honored. In the library situation particularly, the changeover from manual system to computerised system, habitual situation to totally unknown environment create the apprehensive mind. Sometimes the persons resist the proposed change.

Management leaders can overcome resistance both from inside and outside the library through the following ways:

1. Frequent and honest communication throughout the organisation about the change to explain its purposes, to reduce uncertainty, and to show how the change will contribute both to the greater good of the elientele and the community and to personal needs of the library personnel.
2. Genuine and widespread participation in the change process so that people in the organisation feel they have a voice in designing the change and can exercise some control in its implementation.
3. Effective training programmes that enable people to learn why the change is necessary, what it requires from them, and what it means for them personally.

These three approaches are very helpful in reducing any kind of resistance to major change. These three approaches will be very effective if the management leader creates an organisational climate that not only accepts change and the adjustments required accompanying it as normal, inevitable in library situation and exiting, but actively seeks and welcome change also as the source of new opportunities for self-development and service to the community. The entire organisation learns how to achieve the goals of the organisation in the most dynamic and innovative way. The change is required in the fundamental nature of the organisation and a new paradigm of service. No aspect of the activities, operations, programmes and management of the organisation remains untouched.

The crucial concern of management leadership is making the right changes at the right time to improve the organisation's effectiveness. Effective leaders tend to be extremely sensitive to opportunities for change. The management leader can facilitate the process of change by taking the following steps.

1. The prime responsibility of the leader is to define the reality to make everybody understand regarding the inevitability of change in the organisation for the interest of the development of the organisation. This is especially important when the leader is trying to effective change, because the great enemy of change is the mentality of library authority and library personnel to want to perpetuate the existing condition, thereby implicitly denying a change is needed. The leader has to identify the need and has to convince all the people that change must be the reality for the future.

2. Effective management leaders are great believers in participation. The leader should know what role each person should play and how people can interact most effectively with each other to achieve what needs to accomplished. The leaders select the team that will be responsible for implementing change and create a setting in which team members can work well together. They establish a common framework of values and expectations. They appoint to positions of team leadership those already strongly committed to the change. They take the responsibility to implement the changing process on schedule and act accordingly. The leader should listen to all points of view, take steps for participation and cooperation in planning and implementing the change process.

3. At the planning stage, organisational stage and various stages of implementation of the change

process, final decision has to be taken by the leader. Effective leaders take all the information regarding all the programmes and their latest progress as well as constraints, if any. They use their best judgement and intuition, make critical decisions at every point to shape the future of their organisations. It is the leader who bears ultimate responsibility for the success or the failure of decision. Good judgement for taking a decision is an amalgam of good and right information, insightful analysis, foresight and courage. It is the most critical role of the management leader.

The management leaders can develop their organisations and can put new life to the organisations by developing the human resources in the most effective way. They have to build their team to guide the workforce in proper direction. They have to earn the trust, support and loyalty of their staff. The leadership can be inspiring and result-oriented by performing the following tasks:

1. Building the purpose-oriented staff team,
2. Igniting the passion of everyone involved,
3. Designing the right kind of organisation and developing effective operating procedures,
4. Creating an organisational culture with common values, attitudes, and expectations,
5. Developing a successful management-staff relationship,
6. Encouraging top performance and ensuring that performance is carefully reviewed and good performance rewarded, understanding issues for better performance and creating accountability and responsibility,

7. Fostering growth in the organisation so as to increase its capacity to make a difference in the community.

The vital task of the leader is to help the organisation reach a new, higher level of service to its elientele and the community. The performance in totality is actually accomplished not only by the leader but by the team the leader develops for the purpose. A strong team in an organisation is one in which team members have diverse skills and backgrounds but share common goals, are committed to a common cause, provide mutual support, and communicate well with each other. The fine art of team building requires selecting the right people with the right skills, positioning them so that they can make their greatest contributions, and fostering their sense of mutual responsibility for achieving the mission and vision of the organisation.

Effective leaders want the entire organisation to have an integrity of its own and ability to provide value to its elientele. The passion of the leader elevates the spirit of the staff members, and builds commitment for collective effort. The vision of the leader should be conveyed to the team members through collective interactions. The staff members can give their loyalty and support to their leader, but that support has to be earned by the leader.

Organisations can develop through the activities of the human resource, with distinctive competence that they can do better than anyone else. Peter Senge observes in his "The Fifth Discipline" (1990) that, "organisations where people continually expand their capacity to create the results they truly desire, where new and expansive patterns of thinking are nurtured, where collective aspiration is set free, and where people are continually learning how to learn together." Within the organisation there should be a free flow of information, frequent feedback and consultation on all major issues and an openness to change. Organisations should be designed to make full use of information and communication technologies by broadening their access to information both from inside and outside the organisation. These technologies can also support new service delivery systems.

Every organisation has a structure of its own, but it cannot sustain for long effectively without the organisational culture of its own through shared beliefs, values, identity and sense of belonging of its own workforce. The prominent part of the leader's task is to shape the organisational culture so that the total workforce contributes to the fulfillment of the objectives and goals of the organisation. The organisational culture reflects in mutual support, loyalty at every level, mutual trust. All these can be created by the leader with his vision, management principles, organisational capability and personal integrity. The leader has to nurture individual and collective growth. He should do everything possible to help the library personnel increase their knowledge, improve their skills, expand their outlook and work towards higher levels of performance. In "The Good Society" (1991) R. Bellah states that leaders need to develop organisations "that are functioning well, that give the individuals within them a purpose and an identity, not through molding them into conformity but through challenging them to become active, innovative, responsible, and thus happy persons because they understand what they are doing and why it is important".

Certain personal characteristics help the leaders to go through both congenial atmosphere as well as adverse situations. To get the best results the leaders should 'listen carefully to the critics and seek common ground, delegate responsibility to colleagues upon whom one can rely, create improved systems for accountability, produce changes that make a difference, and demonstrate through personal commitment and passion the worth of organisation and its programs'.

Accountability of the management leader is a prime factor in his own organisation as well as in the society at large. It involves the issues of professionalism, morality, organisational performance, and responsiveness to the needs and expectations of his colleagues as well as the authorities. These are real obligations to his leadership, the organisation and the profession. It has been defined by K.P. Kearns (1996) as stated "Accountability involves preserving the public trust - being able to account for the organization's implied promises to its constituencies by pursuing its stated mission in good faith and with defensible management and governance policies... People want to know not only that we are doing what we promised to do, or what we are legally obligated to do, but what they expect us to do, what they want us to do, what they think we should do."

The management leaders are answerable to their authorities, colleagues and clientele and vulnerable to criticism. Effective leaders establish mechanisms to ensure that high standards are applied throughout the organisation. These are checks and balances, performance audits, formal reporting procedures, strict implementation of organisational policies, and performance evaluation. All these mechanisms depend on ability to measure effectively organisational performance and leadership success.

The prime attribute of the management leaders is the professional competence. The advice of Confucius, the great Chinese philosopher to a leader of his time is most appropriate to our time also. He told "Do not worry about holding high position, worry rather about playing your proper role." The management leaders must play their proper roles. Professional competence signifies that these roles are well executed with great integrity and in the best interests of the organisation and the community it serves.

Professional competence of the management leader can only be evaluated qualitatively. The following parameters can be considered for performance evaluation of the management leader.

1. The leader should develop and secure commitment to an effective vision and mission statement for the organisation,
2. He should develop and implement an effective strategy for the future development of the organisation,
3. He should maintain high ethical standards throughout the organisation and should serve as a role model for the staff members,
4. He should exercise good judgement in decision-making,
5. He should organise and manage the affairs in practical and meaningful way,
6. His performance should be more than the expectations of the authorities as well as his subordinates,
7. He should make other leaders grow to leave a legacy.

The performance of the leader can be evaluated by fulfillment of the above parameters and to what extent these are applicable to the leader, by authorities, by colleagues.

12

Human Resource Strategy

Information and communication technologies are reshaping the work environment, and the library personnel must have not just technical training but information management skills. In a computerised work place the activities and operations are identical and equally computer-dependent for top level management to juniormost subordinates. Therefore, changes need to occur in library work schedules and activities like typical corporate human resource organisations. Information technology is not just an area of and application of library and information services. The pervasive use of information technology and reliance upon it have become a part of all human activities.

From factory floor to research institutes, unlimited communication and data transfer, information resources and their updatedness - in all spheres of activities the use of computers, databases and telecommunication networks have become a way of life. Information transfer, storage, and their appropriate use have changed the activities of large corporate organisations to smallest business house, top executives to smallest personal use. "Information worker" is not an academic label restricted to library and information field, it is a description, to varying degrees, of the individuals in any life activity. Information is not a resource with tangible entity, but it is the most essential resource for most of the human activities today.

In the information age, whatever may be the synonyms, the nature of the work is being transformed, as the demands upon the workers, environmental change in workplace, and the quality of the productivity. The working people are not just technical, they must have information management skills. The workplace is not limited both in space and time and the productivity does not depend on formal processes, depend very much upon individual and collective motivation to succeed. Information work and information workers are inherently mobile, and their mobility is never limited to "job of the office". The prime concern of the management of any organisation is the complexity of proper recruiting, channelising the development of human resource, and continuing improvement of expertise and skill in their specialised activities and operations.

The transformation of work culture from manual to electronic entails transformation of human resources in motivation, attitude to face challenges, new skills, effective expertise, aptitude for innovation and achieving result. It can be done by ensuring the availability of talented personnel. Usually the attention of library management and authority is drawn to senior management evaluation and succession planning including selection of top executives. The library authority should be serious to induct talented and result-oriented persons because they assume strategic importance in computerised work situations. The library authorities must make plans and take decisions for encouraging necessary transformation of human resource, and must induct new employees who can accept the challenge and transform the library and information services to the desired new height.

A panel of experts with Peter Drucker, Judy Bardwick, Marvin Bressler and Dave Ulrich has developed recently (1998) a vision of the future of human resource management and the characteristics of a successful human resource executive. The human resource management strategy of an organisation must change to its very core. Human resource management must be a line function, not a staff department activity. Peter Drucker is of the opinion that human resource "should be the agency for actively deploying employees - for continuously matching people and jobs to the benefit of both the individual and the corporation."

Successful activities, operations and services can be possible through perspective planning, designing organisational infrastructure and flowcharting of operational system but the best result can be achieved when staffed with the right mix of people and their skills. The persons who are the right choice for such an environment, know their business and capability are not available easily. They have prepared themselves for interesting and important work to do. They like to stay happy being genuinely productive.

Usually the placement function of human resource often ends with a new employee's first job assignment. After that the person is left to the structural ladder of the organisation either to go up or to be shunted somewhere. In modern human resource management policy the strategy is that human resource is really resource when they find the "line function". In line function every individual is considered to be the key person for the core activities to be performed, ensuring adequate supply of the most essential input to productive human capital. Thus, the human resource strategy is to change the role of individuals in an organisation.

Human resource management policy must emphasise on the human nature of the persons employed, not just personnel administration. The routine administrative tasks should be given to persons not essentially productive information scientists. In this way, human resource understanding will encourage human responses and will represent the human element to work. Thus, they will add extraordinary new value to the organisational work culture.

The information systems designers can develop new work patterns that are truely productive and that maximise the value of human talent. It has been experienced in so many situations that technological projects, in particular, most often fail for lack of far-reaching technological vision and for non-technological reasons. Traditional method of thinking and conventional way of administration cannot cope with the technological advancement. It needs deployment of human resource effectively to adopt technological practices that increase motivation and performance of the workforce. The line managers can use assistance in the human factors of work. The inefficiency of an organisation causes due to human factors, not much due to operational and financial reasons.

Human resource must concentrate on "deliverables, not doobles." It is not important what activities the people perform, but what results have been achieved and how the goals have been reached. Any organisation really need the human resource attitude - not just passive support function, but a point of view on the critical issues of people and organisation, and a willingness to educate people, to push that point of view, and to make results happen.

The human resource strategy leads to the transformation of human resource. The human resource managers must have the following attributes,

* Leadership and courage,
* Line experience to decide the performance strategy,
* Knowledge in computer application, appropriate software application, information and communication technology,
* Expertise in psychology, change of work culture and change of management techniques,
* Knowledge of human resource management and strategy,
* Personal credibility of human resource executive to play both the roles of collaborator and peer on the executive team.

The most vital issue of the technological workplace in an organisation is the necessary and inevitable convergence of people and technology management. The greatest challenges of human resources management strategy involve deploying and developing the workforce with knowledge of appropriate technology, and accommodating their technology-enabled patterns of work. The greatest challenges and crucial issues of information technology implementation are the human issues. These involve creating productive person-machine combinations and motivating people to work and work together in the new ways enabled by new technological tools. The strategic importance of both human resource and information technology is at an all-time high. This strategic role leads to the ongoing challenge to keep pace with performance standard and to focus every service activity on delivering appropriate results.

Human resource management strategy and information technology together with human capability can create the ideal and most effective service fabric that the end-users demand. These can act as real change agents for developing more crucial and productive work processes, more robust inter-organisational working relationships, and ultimately the network of development.

INFORMATION TECHNOLOGY WORKFORCE

Information technology is the education, study, design, process development, implementation, support, job operation and management of computer-based information system using computer hardware system and appropriate software applications. Information technology workers help ensure that computer systems with all the peripherals work well and the information results are specific enough and updated with the help of application software. Whether hardware manufacturing or software development, large organisation or personal requirement, information technology workers are needed to keep the installation and operations in proper working order.

According to industry experts most information technology workforce fall into four broad categories:

1. Computer scientists
2. Computer engineers
3. System analysts, and
4. Computer programmers

Human resource managers responsible for recruiting information technology personnel increasingly must become trained with the functions and operations of the myriad job titles now in vogue. Some of them are given below. Persons required for:

* Database generation and inward transfers,
* Database management,
* Information systems operators or analysts,
* Interactive media specialists,
* Programmer and analyst,
* Software engineer,
* Hardware maintenance operators,
* Software developer,
* Software support expert,
* Technical support personnel
* Network specialist

All these persons cannot be hired for all the time. Therefore, library employees must be trained as far as practicable. Human resource managers should play a vital role in the training programmes, but usually training programmes, in-service training and orientation to newly introduced technology and services are not in their job descriptions. Therefore, they are focused on recruitment of new employees and not on building a new workforce.

There is also a need to improve the quality of information technology education and training. Those who get short courses and periodic exposure to fragmentary computer and information technology courses or refresher courses are not competent to work as information technology workforce because of their fragmentary knowledge, incomplete training and lack of skill in technological environment. There is an ever - expanding distance between the information centres require the actual work situation. Libraries and information centres require the persons who are properly qualified with intensive education and proven skill to fit to their needs but the persons already employed persons aspiring employment are often ill-suited to deal with state-of-the-art technology, which continues to advance while students are still learning about yesterday's technology. Another problem is the person's unfamiliarity with corporate culture. The persons might have computer skills but they have no idea regarding library automation software, library and information technology requirement, and library and information activities and operations. There is no proper educational facilities for specific library and information technology area. It is a great problem for appointing library personnel.

In large libraries, information centres, R and D organisations and other similar organisations there should be human resource managers or executives and they must become knowledge brokers. They should become as critical as information technology experts, because they have to chart strategies to build that knowledge and make it used in the real life operations. For this purpose there must be coordinated efforts among library and information centres, teaching institutions, university departments and sponsoring bodies offering library and information technology training.

The information technology workers need continual development even with degrees, certificates and training. Information technology professional need to stay updated on the dramatic changes they encounter every time. Rapid technological changes and new technological innovations make knowledge and skill obsolete faster than before. It requires inquisitiveness and intellectual stamina to remain current and updated. They must not become fatigued trying to keep up. As learning professionals they must accept the challenge to help people assimilate information and transfer it quickly in applicable ways. Learning professionals including human resource trainers, can contribute to the success of creating information technology environment by giving emphasis on how people learn and apply the knowledge and skill in real life situations.

The stunning power of ubiquity in computerised environment and the multifaceted, multi-directional and multi-layered capability of information technology have made the management and productivity most efficient, most flowness and most timely. When Edison domesticated electricity, since than no technology revolutionised the human work and efforts and life the way the computer has made. Computers touch every aspect of human life activities, domestic, industrial, educational, entertainment, scientific and technological research, and so on. Charles Wiseman, a professor at the Theseus Institute, a French business school, whose curriculum focuses on the relationship between management and technology observes that "The original application of IT was to automate the obvious. But because it is so flexible, it began to affect power relationships. The distribution of information, and even competitive advantage". The computer power and technologies are available, but sometimes there is a question mark regarding their application and productivity. Technology, however powerful it may be, cannot work if there is no management and no useful workforce.

An economics professor of the Royal Institute of Technology in Stockholm refers to a report by J. Westerman made sometime in 1768 under the topic "On the Inferiority of Swedish Compared to Foreign Manufacturers because of a Slower Work Organization." The focus of investigation was a comparative study of the production of Swedish shipyards and ceramics and the production of the same by their British and Dutch counterparts. The result of his investigation was that the Swedish industries and their counterparts in these two countries used essentially the similar machineries and "the Brits and Dutch had no advantage in technology - but the Swedish suffered because the human side of their enterprise was less well-conceived." Machinery alone cannot be productive unless the workforce or the human factor is equally productive. This was a fact in the middle of the eighteenth century, as on record, as well as it is a fact at any point of human history. The change and advancement of technology, however, powerful it may be, cannot be effective and productive if human nature, its motivation and direction are not properly changed and directed to the optimum level.

Terry Neill, Head of change management practice at Anderson Consulting observes that, "Ten, 15 years ago, we caused as many problems as we fixed. We learned that inserting the technology will not of itself do something wonderful." The most important factors are leadership, courage, and the "concerns of your people". The management problem posed by the computers is not just technology, it is also created by the people responsible for its application. These two factors are so interlinked, so pervasive and so essential that the management has to think about strategy and information technology together. In information technology area the business cannot be done just by "top - down, boss - led change". The technology personnel are the ruler of the information age, what is received as information and what is served as information, both are intangible. The expertise of the people and the knowledge of information are the prime factors.

The growth and specific applications of services are more valuable than tangible objects. The electronic systems of a car costs more in comparison to the steel used in it; microchips are not valuable because of the new materials, that is sand, but because of the elegance of their design and the intellectual sophistication of the machines that made them. Therefore, competitive advantage is increasingly derived from the capability to handle, organise, integrate and deliver the knowledge. All these can be done by computers, technologies, communication, networking and the myriad world of electronic magic.

Computer or the electronic magic cannot perform jobs by itself. The machines are tireless, these are never bored, these can store, process, transfer, collate, retrieve any quantum of information and records, can work and operate unimaginably fast and can get global access on finger tips. At the same time the machines can help enormously the persons at work by relieving them of mechanical, repetitive, tiresome, monotonous paper work and self-destroying lifeless work schedules. Machines also give essential human elements - motivation, challenging attitude, cooperation, ambition, teamwork, sympathy, top-bottomless human endeavour, and building human relationship.

In is generally believed in our society that human relationships were more humane in by-gone days and in modern times people are very much machine-dependent, and with more machines we are becoming mechanical. And the most powerful machines, the computers are breaking the human relationships as well as social relationships.

Thomas A. Stewart (1995) writes "Computers, far from dehumanizing people, are adapting to our idiosyncratic humanity. Picture Frederick Taylor, the guy with the stop watch, doing time- and- motion studies... Fast -forward today: Anderson Consulting has a "usability lab" designed to uncover problems in the software it writes. In the portable version of the lab, the firm comes to your office, aims a camera at your computer and one at you, and records your Keystrokes. A consultant watches, taking notes as you fumble, curse, or hit the help button. It looks like Taylor with a camcorder but for one crucial difference: Taylor stepped forward to tell the worker how to become more like a machine; the Anderson consultant goes back to tell the engineer how to make the machine more humane". Man-machine relationships are truely people-machine relationships.

Information technology is totally different from other technologies, in the sense that the more sophisticated it gets, the easier and more useful it becomes, even for the non-experts. With a short training and with the help of the manual an interested person can use the technology. Mel Horwitch, professor of management at the Theseus Institute observes "Technology will cause a resuscitation of general management in the old tradition". Thomas A. Stewart states, "mystifying in itself, it is a great demystifier, vastly increasing a manager's ability to move among and interpret the multiple worlds of finance, customers, and technology. It is democratizing". Horwitch says, "The whole point of network is that people are important".

Human resource is most crucial and vital resource in any organisation. Technology, with the latest developments, facilitates the human resource to get the best of it for the benefit of the human society. The "best" can be achieved only by the human resource with its best utilisation. Best utilisation of human resource depends very much upon the human resource strategy in the organisation from time to time.

STRATEGIC PLANNING

In the present library environment the librarians must act proactively and creatively to develop effective future of the library through the strategic planning of human resource. The principles, processes, and mind set of strategic planning is a productive endeavour for all types of libraries and information centres. The library management should think strategically and should plan formal strategic planning efforts for the library.

Strategic planning is an active, ongoing process and way of thinking that concentrates human resource in areas that are most productive. It is a tool of leadership that can build consensus among all the persons in the library and promote the proper understanding of and commitment to the goals of the library. It must also be consistent with the mission and goals of the parent organisation. The future of the library should be anticipated and the human resource strategies should actively meet the future. The strategies require continuous review and updating. The most important aspect of strategic human resource planning should be embedded in library planning, operations and the library culture.

Organisational designs can be used to encourage the development of creative structures. Organic structures, in contrast to hierarchical structures, allow for adaptation to planned change. These designs may be the use of task forces, small working groups, temporary work groups for specific activities. These are all flexible structures that operate for adaptation to change. These groups can respond to a crisis, experiments with various projects, identify problems, propose solutions more quickly and efficiently than conventional hierarchical set up. The activities of these types of groups can encourage entrepreneurship in the organisation and can faster creativity avoiding bureaucratic constraints on the process of change. The library personnel, thus, can be transformed into human resource for designing and implementing new concepts.

The essential factor is the coordination of activities in its totality if the work of such groups is to benefit the organisation. Thomas J. Peters and Robert H. Waterman observe that managers need to look for ways to encourage the development of spontaneous processes that can cope with unanticipated changes in the environment. Karl Weick observes that "An organisation that sees itself in novel images, images that are permeated with diverse skills and sensitivities, thereby is equipped to deal with altered surrounds when they appear. To bring creativity and innovation into the organisation, managers need to take pleasure both in the process and in the outcome".

The critical steps to improved performance in organisations are the empowerment of library personnel and their meaningful involvement at all levels of the library. Roger D. Evered and James C. Selman have explained this philosophy in their description of a new paradigm for the relationship between senior level and subordinate staff. They describe this the "acknowledge- create- empower" paradigm and suggest that its fundamental beliefs "have to do with rethinking own thoughts, aligned purpose, commitment to accomplishment, collaboration, involvement, mutual support, individual growth - in short, enabling the people in a group or team to generate results and to be empowered by the results they generate."

The authors acknowledge that "acknowledge - create - empower" paradigm is a difficult one, but they propose that the role of manager as a coach is the appropriate strategy for the transition from hierarchical to this new paradigm. The new meaning of coaching is one of a committed partnership. They describe in this way "... a coach is some one who has an ongoing, committed partnership with a player/performer and who empowers that person, or team, to exceed prior levels of play/ performance." The heart of coaching in this context is the relationship between the manager or leader and the staff members.

Maureen Sullivan states the essential elements of this meaning of coaching are:

1. Partnership, mutuality, relationship
2. Commitment to producing a result and enacting a vision
3. Compassion, generosity, nonjudgemental acceptance, love
4. Speaking and listening for action
5. Responsiveness of the player to the coach's interpretation
6. Honoring the uniqueness of each player, relationship, and situation
7. Practice and preparation
8. Willingness to coach and be coached
9. Sensitivity to "team" as well as to individuals
10. Willingness to go beyond what's already been achieved.

The role of the manager as coach and guide, and the acknowledge-create empower paradigm offer the management a means to create the future service design and its implementation to achieve the goals of the organisation through the best performance of its human resource. The human resource, as a whole, assumes their responsibility for their performance by developing their full potential being committed to excellence. The library personnel must have greater involvement, in the problem-solving and decision-making activities, self-responsibility for development to achieve the desired excellence.

Edward E. Lawler in his "High-involvement Management" (1986) describes the fundamental principles about the library personnel in a successful organisation. These principles signify the effective and meaningful participation of the human resource in the library. These are stated below:

HUMAN RELATIONS

People should be treated fairly and with respect. People want to participate. When people participate, they accept change. When people participate, they are more satisfied and committed to the organisation.

HUMAN RESOURCE

People are a valuable resource because they have ideas and knowledge. When people have input in decisions, better solutions are developed.

Organisations should make a long-term commitment to the development of people because it makes them more valuable to the organisation.

HIGH INVOLVEMENT

People can be trusted to make important decisions about their work activities. People can develop the knowledge to make important decisions about the management of their work activities. When people make decisions about the management of their work, the result is greater organizational effectiveness.

This general set of principles would effectively support a strategy for greater involvement of library personnel making them true human resource in the organisation. This set of principles articulates the organisational philosophy and values proven to be a critical step for successful organisations. The individual library and its human resource should articulate its own set of principles and their applications. It is essential that the library management and the total human resource would act in accordance with these principles with all sincerity and seriousness.

The coaching role of the leaders, the principles for "high-involvement management" and the "acknowledge-create-empower" paradigm suggest a set of critical behaviours for the management leaders in the new environment. Edward E. Lawler suggests that, "The key positions need to be staffed by leaders. Traditional managerial behaviors are not needed... Leadership, however, is needed to provide a sense of purpose and direction as well as to shape the organization's culture and decision processes." For the leaders, it is essential to believe that the library personnel are capable members of the library who are committed to its success and who will work towards the success.

Leaders should carry out their activities and everyday responsibilities having on-going interactions with the library personnel. Leaders create many opportunities for the subordinates to participate in decisions and also to exercise leadership. They encourage a shared leadership in which the personnel assume a mutual responsibility for high performance. The leaders articulate a vision of the organisation that provides a sense of direction and purpose.

This vision is most important to all the library

personnel at all levels of the library. The management leader provides the vision for the library as a whole. The departmental heads and the sectional heads define the vision in their respective areas that is consistent with the central vision. The vision guides the leaders and the staff in setting goals and objectives of performance. It also describes the future programmes and activities of the library in near future and far future.

The shared leadership of library personnel is recognised as an evolutionary process and the management leaders require careful attention to the developmental levels of the library personnel. The members of the staff are outwardly seen as different individuals that they are, but they are at varying levels of development to be qualified as appropriate human resource. The management leader helps each person to perform at their current level of development as well as continuing to develop their skills and effectiveness. While the staff develop, management leaders gradually share more responsibility. As the new skills are learned and new technologies are operational in the library, greater independence of operational activities in encouraged and more responsibilities are delegated.

Paul Hersey and Kenneth K. Blanchard suggest the model of "Situational Leadership" in four different, but progressive continuum leadership styles for corresponding continuing developmental levels for library personnel. In the early stages of leader/staff relationship, the appropriate style of the leader is a highly directive one to match the needs of the new, inexperienced staff member who has limited understanding of organisational goals and who requires considerable structure and direction from the leader. As the staff member develops proper understanding and commitment to the objectives activated in the work, gains experience, assumes greater responsibility, and becomes a competent performer, the leader gradually moves through the continuum of styles to the fourth stage, the leader as developer.

Problem-solving should be made through the new approach. Problems are seen as opportunities for the staff and the management leaders alike to learn and to develop their skills and capabilities. The increased complexity in the work and the systems designed for the accomplishment of this work have created new problems, many of which are quite complex. The leader recognises that problem-solving is both a technical process and one that furthers the development of those who participate. When things go wrong or failures occur, the leader analyses the situation and makes attempts to understand the reasons. This is done for the purpose of learning, and continuing learning discovers the ways of problem-solving.

The management leader should empower the library personnel by encouraging self-responsibility and shared responsibility by giving work assignments. When the specific responsibilities are delegated, performance expectations should be clearly stated and set by the supervisor and the staff mutually. The library personnel should know and understand the standards for competence levels of performance. Every person should be encouraged to assess their own performance on an on-going basis and to take corrective actions as necessary. When they are not able to take such actions, the management can help them. They should be encouraged to take decisions when they are able to take. Such empowerment represents a shift away from a dependent relationship to one of interdependence.

The delegation of responsibilities should be based on a careful assessment of the person's skills and capabilities for performing the work. When responsibilities change the supervision should monitor the person's ability to perform new tasks, performance problems should be addressed as soon as they occur. The supervisors should understand the performance problems, should encourage the staff to solve the problem and should provide support and guidance wherever needed.

The effective management leader is a skilled communicator by following a variety of methods for formal and informal sources. He should regularly interact with all the persons by sharing information as well as receiving it. Any major decision or any change of workflow should be announced well before they are implemented, and ideas and staff reactions should be encouraged. The new leadership paradigm requires different organisational structures that are flexible and open to change. The library personnel require appropriate work environment, timely decisions and effective performance to achieve the goals of the library. Decision-making at the lower levels suggests fewer management levels, increased participation in problem-solving and decision-making by groups or teams with participation and shared responsibility.

David L. Bradford and Allan R. Cohen suggest that special groups should be constituted with "mature, shared-responsibility teams" that would provide for coordination of the group works and high-quality solutions to complex problems. The work groups can work in specific areas as self-managing teams in effective structure of increasing human resource commitment to quality performance. Clearly recorded and meaningful performance goals, keeping good standards in activities, successful individual performance, highly motivated human resource and planning for future improvement and development are the most crucial factors for making human resource management strategy.

Honest, open and clear communication on the part of both supervisors and subordinates at all the management levels is critical for proper and accurate assessment of performance and deployment of improved human resource. The library management must be "high-involvement" management group.

Management leaders as well as library personnel should keep abreast of developments and new trends in the library and information scenario in the global perspective, its parent organisation, the user community and beyond. The external information in the field and the external environment can guide internal decisions. Change is complex, but it is challenging opportunity. It is also evolutionary process that should be managed. The responsibilities for managing the desirable change underway in library and information centres rests with the management leaders. The library personnel with responsibility and involvement are a vital resource. Meaningful participation, empowerment and the on-going development of the library personnel at all levels are the critical tasks of human resource management.

13

Learning Support Systems

The global information society of the new era is the knowledge-based society. The technological innovations, challenges to face the societal change and the impact of such changes in all life activities are the biggest concern of the people used to traditional life style with conventional systems. The information and communication technologies have changed significantly the development paradigm. The technologies are so pervasive that the demarcation between information-rich and information-poor is not so easy to define. Both the conditions can coexist even in a particular geographical region or in a particular society. The technological development has reduced the gap between information-rich and information-poor societies and it has been realised that access to accurate, specific and updated information are essential in this gap reduction. In the global perspective the countries are divided in two blocks, developed and developing, in economic terms. It is also easy to identify the countries in similar blocks on the basis of information-rich and information-poor in respect of technological development. At the same time there are information-rich and information-poor segments of societies within countries.

In this context, there is no doubt that human resource management is one of the biggest challenges to be faced as well as to be solved. The availability of new information and communication technologies, the formal acquisition of information and knowledge is no longer limited to particular geographical region. Access to information in real-time from several organisations and from a number of countries is a factual situation.

Human resource management includes also information specialists properly educated through continuing learning systems to serve as the intermediary between information resource and the end-users or the specific target groups. The challenges are major in this area. The information specialists must have the knowledge base and the skills in ensuring global access to information. regardless of the sources and the locations. It is very difficult to achieve the goals. The information specialist must know the location, sources, methods to reach the sources, the search engines, the protocols and the specific information out of bewildering mass of databases. The understanding of the application of technologies in the manipulation, search strategy and transfer of information may be over shadowed by issues of equity of access, fair use, ownership and privacy protection. The identical information resources and databases can be available in different locations having different criteria. The need and purpose of the search for the time being requested by the user will dictate the specific information. The information tools are to be used properly and specifically. The human resource management, in this respect, is a critical challenge both for the individual and for the organisation.

Information technology and communication infrastructure are the vehicles for transfer of specific users' needs and requirements as well as transfer of information, a linkage between sender and receiver on a reciprocal basis from any point to any point and vice versa. All these are the electronic transportation infrastructure. The prime component is the knowledge content which include information in itself, data storage and knowledge bases. Other components associated are data management techniques, information transfer systems and the navigation mechanisms based on search strategies for access to the knowledge bases. Therefore, in networked system there are three crucial components. The knowledge bases are ever-expanding because of continuous explosion in the generation of information and databases, through which the volume of knowledge content is continuously becoming larger and larger.

In addition to the current information, there are the accumulated knowledge bases and information resources generated during thousands of yesteryears in various physical formats in different parts of the world. If all these are in the digitised form, it will be beyond any calculation and imagination. A large section of the information population will be required and a larger period of time will be spent for efficient and effective information and knowledge management techniques, and within this time it will become even larger.

Because of the exponential generation of data, it is essential that every library, particularly larger libraries must have larger data storage and retrieval system. Technological advances in optical storage media have made it possible to make phenomenal increase in the capacities of compact disks. Optical disks with more than 50 Gigabytes are available with the Digital Versatile Disks (DVD). Blue lasers will replace infra-red lasers. Optical disks will be the major store house of database in the networked society. At the same time access time will also be minimised.

Very large database systems require new technology for handling massive data the databases would contain. Fast retrieval of specific data items must be ensured from very large databases. It is also to be ensured that no stored data item remains unretrievable. Storage and retrieval of data have become possible for advancement of computer hardware, software and telecommunication

The chip capability for storage continues to expand. The gigabyte chip is a small wafer of silicon about the size of pinkie fingernail. This new chip can hold really no less than one billion bits of information. Such miniaturisation is at the heart of advances of in storage and retrieval of information in the networked society.

All the information technology components are made up of microchips in different forms. The processing unit, storage, memory, and logic circuitry consist mainly of chips imprinted with electronics. The innovation of smaller and smaller chips resulted in increased computing power. Therefore, hardware designers have more circuitry to use, software programmers have more space in which to write. Each new generation of chips becomes commodities, and the price falls. Thus, more powerful hardware and software become relatively less expensive, there is every indication that the cycle will continue because the largest market in the world is the electronic market.

During the ancient and mediaval periods of the human history supply was scarce, and could not satisfy the demands. The key factor was the supply and the key role players were the suppliers. The scripts, alphabets, the writing materials, the printing processes, the scribes, printing by movable types, printing machines, paper, authors, publishers - had the key roles in the contemporary societies to shape the civilisation and culture of the mankind.

The persons who were the discoverers or inventors were responsible for the supply sources. Later, the persons who were the suppliers or manufacturers and made everything available to the people had the key roles to shape the society and for the advancement of humankind.

At the early phase of scientific and technical inventions, whether steam engine, electricity, telephone, telegraph, and others, the inventors paved the way for supply. the commercialisation of all these inventions for the benefit and convenience of the people created the suppliers, who played the key role that made everything available. Thus, supply was forgotten and suppliers became the key players and got the key roles. Nobody remembers Thomas Alva Edison but the society at large cannot think of living without electricity which is the basic necessity like blood circulation.

From the nineteenth century the whole situation has been changed, when supply was identified with suppliers. The human society got all the items of living in a large quantity and did not bother for supply as before. Everything became commodity and availability became assured. The human society became a consumer market and supply and suppliers became synonymous. Now all over the world the supply is a part of life and everything is available. The people who have the necessary resource can get anything they require.

NEW ERA

In the information and knowledge world all the supplies are given and new supplies are updated almost every hour. No individual can read even the smallest fraction of the knowledge stored all over the world in various physical formats, whether on paper or on electronic media. Information has become a commodity and resource to be utilised for any purpose. Information has become a utility like electricity or transport. We just plug on to get it or get the transport to move on. Information is the greatest utility in all sphere of human life activities. We can switch on and get information at any time, any place and from any part of the world with the help of electronic and communication technology.

Libraries and information centres are the places far storage, service, retrieval, dissemination and access to knowledge-based information in the electronic environment. The traditional role of library personnel has already been changed to information personnel. The role is being very crucial for changing responsibilities because of new innovations in information and communication technologies. It will change further and further.

In such critical situation the role of the library personnel must be changed. The library and information personnel have to keep pace and go at a good pace with the advancement of the technology. The library personnel should not be passive onlooker but they must be active and effective human resource through transforming their motivation, efficiency, attitude to face challenging situation for tne present and also for the future. The electronic environment in the library and information centres is the basic necessity. But just the training in the computer operation for the conventional library activities cannot help the clientele in the best way. The latest advances in information and communication technologies and their applications in library and information areas, particularly knowledge of databases, their locations, identification of information sources, search technology and access to essential and important databases, cannot be learned without specialised learning resources.

TRAINING : LEARNING

At the changeover phase, from manual to computerised, the training of the library personnel is essential for primarily operations of the computers, new job analysis, new job descriptions, manual activities transformed into machine activities. As a whole, there will be a change in activities, operations attitude, work situations. At this stage training means instructions how to do all the jobs, if there is a problem how to solve, how to operate machines and the peripherals, how to get results, and finally how to get the total library activities and operations done for the interest of the clientele. It is also a continuing process, phase by phase, to have operational control over computerised environment to deliver the services.

The objectives of the training are to provide the trainees with specific understanding about the area of training, scope of training, methods and processes of training and finally what should result from the training process. Training implies the instructional procedures to be taught to the persons who do not know how to do the activities, and after the training the trained persons will be able to perform the jobs. Training courses are held both for theoretical and practical knowledge on specific areas for the time being for some persons. The same training course may be held for a different group of people. The same group of persons may get training either for further knowledge or in different kinds of activities. In training a number of persons are trained on specific job areas or operational activities. When the training is over, the phase of instructional schedule for that training in also over.

These are essential differences between training and learning support systems. Training may be for manual

	TRAINING	***LEARNING***
DURATION :	SHORT PERIOD	EVEN LIFE LONG
MAIN PERSON :	INSTRUCTOR OR TRAINER	LEARNER
PROCESS :	TECHNICAL	HIGHLY TECHNOLOGICAL
KNOWLEDGE BASE :	ELEMENTARY	HIGHLY PROFESSIONAL
KNOWLEDGE AREA :	LIMITED TO TRAINING	COMPREHENSIVE
CONTROLLED BY :	TRAINERS	SELF
TOOLS :	TRAINING KIT	ELECTRONIC ENVIRONMENT
PERFORMANCE EVALUATION BY :	TRAINER	SELF
TRAINING AREA :	SPECIFIED JOBS OR ACTIVITIES	WHOLE OF INFORMATION AND COMMUNICATION TECHNOLOGY FIELD
GIVEN BY:	SUPERVISORS AND INVITED TRAINERS	ACADEMIC INSTITUTIONS OR HIGHLY PROFESSIONAL INSTITUTIONS

jobs or technical jobs for a particular objective but learning support is for the life time depending on the will of a person. A table is given on previous page stating the differences between training and learning support, though superficial.

In case of training courses the trainers are usually the supervisors who act as training-in-charge in specific areas and other supervisors can act as trainers depending on the training objectives and training schedules. External resource persons are invited as trainers as and when required according to training course modules and specialisations. Training, as a whole, is primary stage or middle stage education for practical performance activities with theoretical background. Usually training courses are conducted for the junior level posts and middle level positions according to requirements and situations. Training courses enhance the skills as well as technical expertise.

The revolutionary and astounding advancement in electronic technologies and their applications in library, information and communication areas, particularly CD-ROM, fiber optics. multimedia, hyper-text technologies, have changed the internal and external environment of the library and information centres, whether small, medium or large. In such highly technological environment, two situations have become imperative. First, the concept of training to enhance skill and technical expertise is not commensurate with the ever-advancing technological innovations within limited scope of the training. Secondly, in highly sophisticated technological environment the border line between the human resource levels has been almost annihilated. Every person has to work in such environment according to his capability. The concept of training has become obsolete.

In such technological environment group learning

may be there, may not be there but individual understanding and learning is most important factor. Therefore, the supervisors at all the levels may not be competent to train the subordinates. All of them may have to learn as learners The real professional persons with highly technological expertise must be the educators. They may come from the academic institutions, highly professional institutions with proven track record, vendors of the computer systems and other electronic equipment, or finally highly specialised training organisations, vendors of group educators having comprehensive knowledge and adequate experience. They can create the proper learning support systems in library and information centres.

The act of learning is strictly a personal affair and those people with all their support systems are practically neither the teachers nor the trainers. They give only knowledge input, instructional materials, guide the individuals with appropriate highly technological input with problem-solving capabilities. They can tune the human resource in library and information centres with optimum capability and they can assure the required productivity and performance. These specialists, educators in a loose sense, may act as specialist in selection, installation and operation of the computer systems and other systems. It is expected that the specialists of training organisations to know how to access and select the appropriate material and programmes from the overwhelming number of options by selecting the right supplier. They can also help the library authority how to make their own selections. They will also guide the learners in how to use the online search and communication technology.

Such persons, as educators, are expected to support learning that occurs in new ways and with new technology.

They will depend on in-house and outsourced learning functions.

NEW LEARNERS

Human resource development in any organisaton requires training on specific areas, and at different levels of learners and at different levels of management hierarchy levels. Learning support can be primary, advanced level and for high skill and expertise. In all these situations the main functionaries are the learning support providers, those who impart the essential information and skills to be achieved. Trainees are on the receiving end to become trained in a group. The impact of training is evaluated both as a group and as individuals. Their performance during the training courses is evaluated by their attitude, tasks done and activities completed. It is expected that after the training the trainees are prepared for improved efficiency, effectiveness and productivity. The result of the training is to meet job and departmental needs. Therefore, the individuals are not main functionaries.

If a certain type of instruction is the best way to achieve the skill needed for better performance the trainers can provide the instruction. If skill can be achieved through a simple job aid, then the trainers can provide it. The greatest contribution of the trainer is the ability to help achieving skill of the trainees in a particular job and activity. The success of the trainer is to guide the trainees perperly for job performance in specific areas.

In highly technological electronic environment any kind of training, even the best, is considered inadequate to understand the electronic environment in its totality. The electronic environment creates the infrastructure for activities, operations and performance in the integrated way combining a long range of peripherals, equipment, system software and application software, networking protocols, search engines and many other aids. In such environment all the individuals do not work in formal hierarchical order and everybody must know everything by learning everything. Therefore, the main functionaries are the individuals, the learners and not the trainees, through individuals learning. The human resource development in the electronic environment very much depends on individual learning, as opposed to training by trainers.

The information and communication technology literature, books and periodical articles on computer hardware, software and networking, information solution courses, Internet search literature and a large number of hardcopy and electronic publications are available in the market. The manuals, how-to-do-it instructions, and the literature supplied with the electronic devices are also available. All these materials look like learning resources. These can deliver instructions very well constructed. But there is no guarantee that individual learning will take place, even if the instructions and knowledge content are given by the most talented technologists and specialists.

In a library situation, there are specific needs, specific purpose, specific services, particular way of activities and operations, specific search strategy, particular group of end-users with their specific areas of research. The human resource must not be only technocrats. They should have the required academic background, knowledge base in required subject areas and comprehensive knowledge of information resource databases. Everybody will not require everything. All the library and information services should be designed to implement the aims and objectives as well as to achieve the goals of the library and its parent organisation.

Each library has its own nature and character, collection management policy and procedures, housekeeping activities, technical operational systems, service patterns, specialised users services, facilities given to own users and external users, specialisation of subject areas, limitation of technological infrastructue, and such other considerations. Human resource of a library must be developed keeping in mind all these factors. Therefore, every individual of the human resource team has his own role and area of activity and performance, where he is the only performer. But everybody works in the library in the coordinated way having his won role of performance as complement to the total performance of the library. For this reason, everybody is a most important resource to perform the activities at a point of time and there is no substitute. Everybody has his own background, own knowledge base, own skill and expertise as well as his own learning process and learning capability to grasp the knowledge with his own understanding.

Learning through technology by accessing to information sources is essentially a process of self-study. But for many people self-study going through instruction does not work very well. Learning must be supported by human resource learning facilitator who will understand the requirement of each learner about learning to serve in specific work situation with the co-worker and with the technology available in the library. Because self-study is not the best means of delivery for all learners. It would be wrong to blame the learners when they do not succeed.

LEARNING SUPPORT FACILITATOR

To work with advanced technology the conventional training process or courses will not work effectively and meaningfully. The library personnel must give emphasis on learning and individual learning to apply the knowledge appropriately in the work situation. But the concept of training should not be abolished. It should be redesigned and transformed into learning process. The role of trainers or instructors must be played by the new generation of learning support facilitators. They will not impose what to do, but they will help personal learning through inculcating how to do and why it has to be done. This knowledge is facts and concepts such as, steps to a process or system, know-how information to perform a given task effectively.

The capabilities of the library personnel starts with learning support based on the assessment of their abilities to achieve:

* desired results,
* identified critical performance outcomes,
* identification of competitive performance gaps,
* instant service with updated information,
* optimum performance by each person.

To achieving these the following steps should be taken,

* to create performance models based on strategic goals,
* to determine how performance would be measured,
* to identify what the library personnel knew and needed to know,
* to manage the learning support design and development strategy.

The learning support facilitator will do the following activities -

* performance and competency modelling,

* competency assessment,
* resource identification,
* learning development plan,
* on-going evaluation and feedback,
* identification of critical performance results,
* identification of knowledge and skills of the library personnel as assessed against critical results,
* creation of models for learning and development of each individual,
* integration of learning activities into work environment.

The learning support facilitator must identify the gaps between the current knowledge of the human resource and the knowledge and skills needed to achieve critical results. He should collect the data to create learning modules. He should create the performance models and performance development plans for every individual. His work must begin with high-priority learning support areas, and then all the present and future requirements.

BIBLIOGRAPHY

ALA : Staff Development- a practical guide, Chicago, ALA, 1992.

Albritton, Rosie and Shaughnessy, Thomas W.: Developing Leadership Skills-a source book for librarians. Englewood, Colorado, Libraries Unlimited, 1990.

Daft, Richard L. and Lengel, Robert H.: Fusion Leadership, San Francisco, Berrett-Koehler Publishers Inc., 1998.

Drucker, Peter F.: The Practice of Management, New York, Harper & Row, 1954.

French, Wendell L.: The Personnel Management, Boston, Houghton-Mifflin, 1982.

Giesecke, Joan: Practical Help for New Supervisors, Chicago and London, American Library Association, 1992.

Gleuck, William F.: Personnel Management : A Diagnostic Approach, Dallas, Business Publications, 1974.

Heilman, Madeline and Harvey, Hornstein : Managing Human Forces in Organisation, Homewood, III, Irwin, 1982.

Jerris, Linda A.: Effective Employee Orientation, New York, AMACOM, 1993.

Lynch, Mary Jo: Libraries in an Information Society:

A Statistical Summary, Chicago. American Library Association, 1987.

Marshall, Don R.: The Four Elements of Successful Management, New York, American Management Association, 1998.

Rubin, Richard E.: Human Resource Management in Libraries - Theory and Practice, New York, Neal-Schuman Publishers Inc., 1991.

Scholick, Gary P.: Interview Guide for Supervisors, Washington, D.C., College and University Personnel Association, 1988.

Stewart, David and Shamdasani, Prem N.: Focus groups-Theory and Practice, New BuryPark, C.A., Sage Publications, 1990

Stueart, Robert D. and Moran, Barbara B.: Library and Information Centre Management, Englewood, Colorado, Libraries Unlimited Inc. 1993.

Sullivan, Maureen *ed.*: Developing Library Staff for the 21st century, New York, Haworth Press, 1992.

Taylor, Frederick W.: Scientific Management, New York, Harper & Row, 1947

Terry, George: A guide to supervision, Homewood, III, Irwin, 1982

Ziglar, Zig: Top Performance, Old Tappan, N.J., Revell, 1986.

Index